NONPROFIT Z

NONPROFIT Z

BUILDING NONPROFITS IN THE ERA OF TECHNOLOGY

OWEN MAGUIRE

NEW DEGREE PRESS

COPYRIGHT © 2018 OWEN MAGUIRE
All rights reserved.

NONPROFIT Z
Building Nonprofits in the Era of Technology

ISBN 978-1-64137-076-9 *Paperback*
ISBN 978-1-64137-077-6 *Ebook*

"I do not fear computers. I fear lack of them."

—ISAAC ASIMOV

CONTENTS

INTRODUCTION 1

A SITUATIONAL OVERVIEW
1. 8 YEARS LOST 9
2. ON THE OUTSIDE LOOKING IN 25
3. OLD DOG, OLD TRICKS 35
4. GOING BIGGER 45

THE MILLENNIAL INFLUENCE
5. THE MILLENNIAL'S NONPROFIT 59
6. HITCH A RIDE 71
7. INVESTING IN GOOD 81

TECHNOLOGY IN USE
8. BUILDING A COMMUNITY 95
9. WADE THROUGH THE MUD 107
10. BIG DATA, BIG IMPACT 115
11. BLOCKCHAIN FOR GOOD 129
12. HI, HOW MAY I HELP YOU? 139
13. ZIP CODE 2.0 149
14. DELIVERING IMPACT 159
    REFERENCES 169

INTRODUCTION

During my first week at DC SCORES, a youth engagement nonprofit based in Washington, D.C., I was thrown right into the fire. The annual staff retreat and board meeting were held that Thursday and Friday. During the board meeting, the organization's board debated for several hours whether to expand the program to more schools or expand age range of the program within existing schools. Many of the board members, mostly executive-level private-sector workers, were asking what seemed like straightforward questions.

"What is the high school graduation rate of our kids?"

"Does our program really make an impact on reading level and obesity rates?"

But members of our staff simply did not have the data necessary to answer them. The program ran until the end of middle school, but we had no platform or system in place to track the kids afterward. Although increasing literacy and physical health were two of the main goals of the organization, we lacked an effective way to evaluate and track this information.

I was taken off guard that we didn't have the kind of data that the board members were asking for. I had joined the organization having observed that it was well-established, had a clean and user-friendly website, and even had an active social media presence. Yet, the group still hadn't found the technologies that could so clearly solve its problem. It seemed so straightforward.

* *

This is not unusual. Nonprofit organizations are springing up left and right; the sector is growing at a steady pace. According to data cited in October 2015 by the Urban Institute, there were around 1.41 million nonprofits registered with the IRS in 2013, up 2.8 percent from 2003. But, as the industry has grown, it has faced challenges with new technology and related trends. In my conversation with Elaine Turville, a managing director within Accenture's nonprofit practice, she estimated that public sector organizations are about four years behind the private sector in terms of adopting new administrative technology, and the nonprofit sector is an additional four years behind the public sector.

Fundamental nonprofit ideology and constraints due to infrastructure are commonly cited as the barriers to adopting digital. One comment from a survey of nonprofit organizations conducted by Zoe Amar and David Evans stated, "Money that could be spent on digital is needed elsewhere—we don't have the spare resources to boost digital adoption." The humanitarian nature of many nonprofit organizations means that there is little margin for error when tinkering with existing systems that may not be perfect but have been refined over the years.

"Everyone is kind of in the same place in the development community: Everyone wants to be on the cutting edge, but they're making what can be life or death decisions in terms of aid distribution, so they have to get these things right," said Michael Pisa, a policy fellow at the Center for Global Development. The aforementioned nonprofit survey received responses indicating that nonprofits are desperately seeking digital leadership, looking for clear visions of how digital could help them achieve more. Very few charities rated their board's digital skills as high; just 3 percent rated their board as digitally savvy.

Nonprofits also have to confront the deluge of data that many other business sectors have been trying to handle. According to a January 2015 report from Charity Dynamics, 88 percent of nonprofit professionals expect digital fundraising to more than double—from 7 percent of total fundraising to 20 percent—in the next 10 years. All of that digital activity generates data. Yet 57 percent of nonprofits say they are not properly using donor data for marketing strategy and fundraising efforts.

Digital technologies transform how nonprofits connect with clients and create value with their stakeholders. Digital strategies change how we in the nonprofit sector think about our mission and its role in the current marketplace of ideas and services. One study found that 35 percent of surveyed nonprofits use digital technologies but don't have a strategic approach. An additional 12 percent are in the thinking stages of a digital strategy, with 3 percent still struggling to access basic digital tools. Taken together, 50 percent of the charities in the study do not have a strategy focusing on their digital approach and tools. Such a strategy would outline how a nonprofit can take a comprehensive approach to using digital tools and approaches to more efficiently achieve its mission.

* *

Nonprofits face the unique challenge to stay up-to-date on the latest technologies and bridge the chasm between ideation and finding scalable solutions, and are doing so with restricted and risk-averse dollars from donors and grant writers. These institutions face a different set of financial incentives than do private companies or sovereign governments when it comes to deploying new technologies.

This is a key reason why the international development space has lagged behind other sectors in blockchain investment. Despite millions pouring into blockchain and financial technology investment, there remains a "big gap when it comes to deploying blockchain in social impact and governance" areas, said Tomicah Tillemann, head of the Bretton Woods II program at New America.

In this book, I hope to elucidate the reasons behind the nonprofit sector's delay in adoption of technology. For example, an obsession with overhead spending rates has created the starvation cycle that contributes to the lag. But I also offer solutions: I outline a handful of for-profit commercial best practices and how nonprofit organizations can use these resources and tools to invest in technology without donor outcry.

Another focus of this book, and one with which nonprofit organizations have wrestled for years, is how to reach millennials. For-profit companies have cracked the code with digital payments, blockchain, artificial intelligence and virtual reality. I plan to show nonprofit organizations how to integrate these technologies to better capture charitable giving from millennials. Obviously, nonprofits need more than just capital donations; this book also focuses on how to entice millennials to volunteer for your organization or how to expand your impact with the help of digital humanitarians.

Finally, I address use cases of emerging technologies that are fundamentally changing the landscape of social impact. Blockchain seems to be everywhere today, and indeed, nonprofits are looking to integrate it into their work. Not only can they do so by accepting cryptocurrency donations, but the technology can give people an immutable identity. What3Words is a platform that is overhauling the common address system. The technology makes it so that you can pinpoint 9 square meter area of land anywhere on the globe with just three words. Drones, artificial intelligence, social media—the possibilities are endless.

Whether you are currently involved in work at a nonprofit organization or passionate about a cause and thinking about making a difference, I hope this book inspires you to recognize the need for technology in the nonprofit space. In my experience working with nonprofit organizations, I certainly have seen this need. I believe the nonprofit sector can change the world with the help of new and emerging technologies.

PART 1

A SITUATIONAL OVERVIEW

CHAPTER 1

8 YEARS LOST

HOW NONPROFITS MISSED OUT ON THE TECHNOLOGY REVOLUTION

"What we know about charity and the nonprofit sector is undermining the causes we believe in and our desire to change the world," says Dan Pallotta, a humanitarian activist who explains that we expect businesses and nonprofits to use "two separate rulebooks." "Business will move the mass of humanity forward, but will always leave behind that 10 percent of the most disadvantaged and unlucky," he says. "Our social problems are gigantic in scale, our organizations are tiny up against them—and we have beliefs that keep them tiny."

Pallotta is best known for his involvement in multiple-day charitable events like the Breast Cancer 3-Day walks, AIDSRides bicycle journeys, and Out of the Darkness suicide prevention night walks. Today, Pallotta is worried that only one question is used to evaluate a charity: What percentage of my donation goes to the cause versus overhead? "It makes us think that overhead is a negative, that it is somehow not a part of 'the cause,'" he says. "This forces organizations to forego what they need for growth."

Pallotta's nonprofit organizations raised an immense amount of money for their respective causes: over $100 million at each charity. After two of his organizations had their best fundraising years in 2002, they failed and went out of business. Major sponsors pulled out following a slew of bad press that his organization was investing 40 percent of its gross donations into recruitment and customer service. The obsession with overhead spending took down these organizations.

Pallotta had fostered a five-year relationship between his fundraising organization, Pallotta Teamworks, and the Avon Products Foundation, the charitable arm of the Fortune 500 cosmetics company. Pallotta used his Breast Cancer 3-Day concept to increase Pallotta Teamworks' annual breast cancer research grant-making ability from about $5 million per year to $70.9 million per year, raising $194 million net in total for the organization over a five-year period.

However, all of a sudden, Avon said that it no longer wanted to partake in events or activities with Pallotta Teamworks. "They didn't say specifically why—just that they were reviewing all of their fundraising activities. We were floored," says Pallotta. Apparently, the organization valued smaller overhead costs over increased grant writing capabilities.

On August 11th, 2002, the Avon Products Foundation announced its plans for a multi-day walk for breast cancer with full-page ads in major papers across the country, in a way stealing what Pallotta had created. He was outraged—and rightly so: Pallotta's former partner had essentially stepped in as direct competition.

"We owned the events—the name, the concept, the walker lists, and other intellectual property associated with them—so we lined up a new partner to be the beneficiary for the next season. But as a result of Avon's full-page announcements, the new partner that we had lined up backed out—just seven days after the ads ran. The 3-Days were 75% of our business. It was like McDonald's losing the hamburger. There was no time to raise the capital we needed to finance the events' annual cash flow needs. So, on August 23, 2002, we shut our doors, and laid off all 400 employees, including me and my entire leadership team," recalls Pallotta.

Adopting a more business-like approach and investing

in growth allowed Pallotta's organizations to give much more than the publicly accepted fundraising model would have allowed. Pallotta took $50,000 in initial funding for AIDSRides and multiplied it to $108 million. For Breast Cancer 3-Day walks, he took a $350,000 initial investment and multiplied it to $194 million. "[And yet] 350 employees lost their jobs because they were labeled overhead," says Palotta. "This is what happens when we confuse morality with frugality."

This obsession with overhead spending is directly linked to the nonprofit sector missing out on the technology revolution. Nonprofits are unable and unwilling to spend on overhead for fear that donors will cease or pull funding, and so they turn aside opportunities for technological growth. These opportunities and investments may seem expensive up front but that could actually make their use of funds more efficient in the long term.

In a Bridgespan report from 2009, the study introduced "starvation cycle" terminology to the nonprofit world. The report found that nonprofits spend between 10 and 15 percent on overhead, with 15 percent being the popularly accepted spending rate. This overhead level is too low, it starves nonprofits of technological opportunities. According to Bridgespan's research, the average S&P 500 firm spends about 34 percent of its budget on essential behind-the-scenes support. For IT companies, it's more like 78 percent, the report notes. Most 21st-century nonprofits require the same kind of tech firepower but are constrained by their spending models, putting them years behind in technological capabilities.

Keeping the sector's investment in technology low is the view that nonprofits are not allowed to try new things or experiment to innovate. Pallotta says nonprofits buy into this idea because of how quickly news outlets jump on stories of failure, "Nonprofits are reluctant to attempt any brave, daring new fundraising endeavors, because they're scared their reputations will be dragged through the mud." This fear kills innovation and makes it difficult for these organizations to invest in new or emerging technologies. If nonprofits can't try new things and grow, how can they possibly hope to tackle problems on the global scale?

The private sector has been able to try new things. Think of companies like Amazon, which use drones to deliver goods; a nonprofit can deliver much-needed supplies in the same way with the same technology, right? Most nonprofits are lagging behind in adopting new and useful technologies. When they are deterred from trying new things, in this age of innovation and revolution, their systems quickly become obsolete. How can nonprofits hope to create impact when the organization can't function properly in the modern world?

There are a few other factors that contribute to this lag in administrative technology investment. They revolve around some of the key distinguishing factors that come with the nonprofit classification. First, nonprofit organizations operate on the basis of mission, not profit. Private organizations can shape and develop their structure to maximize profit, but nonprofits seek to achieve their mission to the greatest extent possible, regardless of structure. If an organization's mission is to empower Latino students, it is going to do its best to develop its skills in delivering that outcome, which divests resources and funds that could potentially go to technology. Second, most nonprofit business models involve little to zero operating revenue. Nonprofits receive their working capital from outlets such as individual donations, grants and corporate partnerships.

However, these cashflows usually come with restrictions. Foundations and other grant writers usually fund very specific programs or divisions within a nonprofit that align with the mission of that fund or organization. So, nonprofits do not have absolute discretion when it comes to spending and investment.

I talked to Kevin Barenblat, co-founder of San Francisco-based tech nonprofit accelerator Fast Forward about the importance of mission and how it relates to technological investment.

Kevin points out that similar to corporations in the private sector, nonprofit organizations have core competencies in the delivery of services or planning and execution of events. However, nonprofits do not aim to extract the most revenue possible from the people to whom services are provided; rather, they want to provide the service to as many people as they possibly can given their current capital.

Nonprofits have traditionally been grassroots-type efforts. For many years, these organizations have found that the most impactful services are those delivered in person, face to face. Think about soup kitchens, where volunteers contribute by physically serving food.

As a result, all development and investment has not been about changing the way the service is provided; nonprofits still ladle soup the same way they did 10 years ago. Rather, they focus on growing their volunteer network or expanding the community of people they serve.

This process mostly involves storytelling. Storytelling is a key aspect of nonprofit strategy, whereby word of mouth and written testimony attract both volunteers and beneficiaries. Investment in storytelling and physical tools to better provide the service—like trucks, tents and tables—has sapped the funds for grassroots organizations to acquire new and more efficient technological systems.

It is insightful to understand that nonprofits spend their small amount of free operating revenue on these kinds of physical and operational purchases. Most of these investments do not provide the kind of long-term benefits that investment in technology would provide, but it is easier to show a donor how spending money on a truck would impact the services provided than how purchasing a new customer relationship management system would.

As mentioned before, Pallotta has personal experience with the stigma of overhead costs within the nonprofit spending model. Pallotta's investment was in advertising, which is indicative of the perception toward nonprofit investment as it hamstrings an organization's ability to invest in and experiment with use cases for new technology.

"We tell for-profits to spend, spend, spend on advertising," he says. Pallotta goes on to explain how that money invested in advertising can lead to dramatically amplified returns. He talks about his own initiatives as an example. Over nine years, more than 182,000 people participated in Pallotta's AIDSRides and Breast Cancer 3-Day events, raising a cumulative $581 million. "We got that many people to participate because we bought full-page ads," says Pallotta. "Do you know how many people we would have gotten if we advertised with fliers in the laundromat?"

Pallotta's experience with advertising is particularly salient to the importance of spending on overhead technological advancement. Pallotta clearly increased his donor base by taking out ads instead of posting flyers. Imagine the kind of reach that he could have achieved had he engaged in social media campaigns rather than paper ads. Investment in social media is often significantly cheaper than is running paper ads, which can reach astronomical costs in some of the more metropolitan cities like New York. In fact, Facebook and Twitter accounts are free. It costs no money to start the campaign, and all the capital set aside for the campaign can be spent on Twitter and Facebook boosting. An organization can pay to boost its posts, which makes it so that its posts appear higher up on social media feeds and reach a larger audience.

One organization that been effective in capitalizing on the power of social media is charity:water, a nonprofit working to make clean water more accessible to people in developing countries. Social media campaigns can help to make your donors feel like part of a group or team, which drives them to donate. To engage its social media following and raise money, charity:water created a "birthday challenge," in which people could accept donations through an online giving platform instead of getting presents for their birthday. Participants would perform a crazy stunt like do a marathon in a speedo, and publicize it through Twitter and Facebook to get more donations from their friends. In 2015 alone, the campaign raised $1.8 billion.

In 2016, 1,060 people campaigned with charity:water's #nothingiscrazy hashtag. This group of campaigners managed to raise nearly $2 billion because the nonprofit encouraged them to access their own social media following and made it cool to post content and engage in peer-to-peer marketing online. Through its follower's followings, charity:water was able to successfully amplify its message. Over the years, the average individual birthday celebrated through this campaign raised $770. Every single one of your donors have birthdays; think about what possibility each of them brings.

The nonprofit was able to capture such a large amount of donations because its social media campaign made giving and joining the effort cool. And the campaign started through the charity:water social media accounts, which are free to set up. The organization says, "We really maintain a platform on about ten social media platforms. We're sort of everywhere we need to be, because it's as simple as a sign-up." Although the sign-up isn't always that simple, and can involve several, sometimes complex steps, the networks provide more than their share of benefits. charity:water, for example, has managed to cultivate 1.5 million Twitter followers and 375,000 Facebook followers. The organization can instantly reach its audience by publishing content on a simple and free platform.

Social media engagement can clearly make an impact on the effectiveness of a nonprofit organization and is crucial for its development. Unfortunately, many organizations are still simply behind the times when it comes to utilizing the technology that is readily available to them.

"The Government sector is about four years behind the private sector. Nonprofit organizations are around another four years behind that."

This was one key statement that I took from my conversation with Elaine Turville, a managing director in Accenture's human services and nonprofit programs, in reference to the adoption of new and emerging administrative technologies and services. Think about some of the leading companies in the private sector; Google, Bank of America-Merrill Lynch and McKinsey & Co. are just some names that come to mind. These companies are constantly adopting and adapting new tools in the workplace. They have to in order to maintain a competitive advantage.

What about your local nonprofits? Many small- and medium-sized nonprofits are still operating with tools from eight years ago. Some organizations still only use services like Microsoft Office or Google Drive. That is often the extent of their tech development. In today's interconnected world, nonprofits need to invest further in technological tools to help them more effectively reach potential donors, volunteers and beneficiaries.

In the past, nonprofits have been exceptionally slow in adopting new administrative technology that might help streamline their programs and impact their mission. Nonprofits need to address this today given the ever-evolving intersection of technology and CRM on donor relation management.

For instance, the shift to mobile payment technology significantly impacts the business decisions of nonprofits. The next generation of donors are major technology users, and increasingly are using mobile devices to purchase, donate and manage funds. This is true here in the United States—where 86 percent of Americans age 18 to 26 own a smartphone—but also abroad. An NPR report identified that 95 percent of transactions in Sweden are digital, and the entire spectrum of businesses accept forms of digital payment.

I know that, personally, I use my phone for most of my transactions. Some transactions still lend themselves to payment technology like credit and debit cards, such as when I purchase a coffee from the local cafe or a shirt that I try on in the store. However, increasingly, I find myself using technology like Apple Pay—Apple's mobile payment service—to buy food items and e-commerce sites like Amazon to buy other products.

I also find myself frequently using the internet capabilities of my phone to make online donations. It can be extremely useful for nonprofit organizations to reach donors on their phones. Millennials are always surfing social media platforms and internet sites on their phones; enabling this generation to both find and make donations on their phones can help nonprofits to capture more donations.

When I have a particular organization in mind, it is almost impossible to find a physical location to donate. Whether that organization simply does not have a location to make a donation, or it is on the other side of the country, it is almost always too difficult and time-consuming to be worth the effort. I have also never written a check. Most millennials haven't; it is very rare that someone of my generation takes a checkbook from the bank or will take the time to go to the post office to mail a check. If nonprofits are to meet the demands of younger generations, mobile payment technology is key going forward.

According to a 2016 NGO Online Technology Report, only 75 percent of nonprofits accept online payments. This should be at 100 percent. Accepting online donations has never been easier, and organizations can at least get set up through Facebook with a few clicks. The Nonprofit Research Collaborative found that "84% of organizations in 2015 saw the greatest growth in charitable gifts received through social media." It is critical that nonprofits adapt to this change in technology. Unfortunately, some nonprofits will continue to resist moving online because they are too scared to spend on overhead or simply because they do not have any unrestricted funding.

Imagine that you're an entrepreneur running a chain of coffee bars and you want to raise capital to open up in new locations. You meet a potential investor, and he says, "I'd love to finance your business, but only the chai latte operation, not the coffee, and only to support drinks you sell in Boston next year." It might sound absurd, but this is the kind of thing that people running nonprofit organizations hear all the time. These strings-attached funds fuel the nonprofit starvation cycle and hobble the sector.

But there is a way to capture unrestricted funding. Nonprofits can foster a better environment for "partner" donations. A partnership is more like a conversation, with funders learning from nonprofits what they need in terms funding priorities. What the impact foundations seek is very complex to achieve, and made more difficult by inflexible funds that restrain nonprofit organizations' ability to innovate. By fostering a greater sense of partnership, nonprofits enable themselves to demonstrate the need for and earn themselves enough capital to invest in the technology to be successful.

In the current landscape, nonprofits struggle to make necessary investments in technology as a result of an obsession with reducing overhead spending rates. This obsession has created a starvation cycle that has hampered nonprofit organizations' abilities to meet the needs of today's beneficiaries in the wake of the technology revolution. Going forward, nonprofit organizations will have to increase transparency to challenge public perception and free up funds. Hopefully, this capital will be used on vital digital tools, such as online payment processors or social media platforms, that can expand impact and help organizations more effectively achieve their mission.

CHAPTER 2

ON THE OUTSIDE LOOKING IN

WHY PEOPLE LOVE TO HATE NONPROFITS

"How the Red Cross Raised Half a Billion Dollars for Haiti and Built Six Homes"

This is the title of a report by Justin Elliott of ProPublica and Laura Sullivan of NPR. The report tackles the American Red Cross and alleges serious shortcomings in the relief agency's aid to Haiti after the catastrophic 2010 earthquake. Exposés are popular news items in mainstream media, and big social impact organizations occasionally draw big press; unfortunately, the story is often one of failure, fraud or deception. The Red Cross story struck a chord with the public, collecting hundreds of comments and inspiring several similar exposés.

Stories of nonprofit wrongdoing easily gain traction and draw widespread attention, even when details have yet to be verified. Social impact organizations are vulnerable to nearsighted criticism, often centered on executive pay and program expenses. The population at large adheres to the belief that nonprofits don't need to and shouldn't spend on overhead. They cling to this belief strongly, and are quick to tear into organizations. While we love to see falsely lauded people or institutions cut down to size, there are some attitudes that are held toward nonprofits that make them more likely targets. We will discuss how these attitudes affect public response to overhead spending.

Much of the negative sentiment generated in the Red Cross piece dealt with the lack of transparency in spending. Without necessary levels of transparency, skepticism about administrative spending and overhead costs quickly turn into criticism and accusations. Anger was only fueled by the pledges of Gail McGovern, the Red Cross' CEO, to "lead the effort in transparency." She had announced, "We are happy to share the way we are spending our dollars."

The Red Cross' public reports offered only broad categories about where the $488 million in donations was spent. The biggest category listed was shelter, at about $170 million; other categories included health, emergency relief and disaster preparedness. The Red Cross had claimed that it helped 4.5 million Haitians. However, an internal evaluation found that in some areas, the Red Cross reported helping more people than even lived in the communities, and in others, double-counting went uncorrected. So, it is clear to see how these public reports offered little to no transparency to donors.

As a result, individuals took it upon themselves to uncover the spending tactics of the Red Cross and other nonprofits. This campaign ultimately turned into an attack on the organization's overhead spending. McGovern told CBS News a few months after the earthquake, "Minus the 9 cents overhead, 91 cents on the dollar will be going to Haiti. And I give you my word and my commitment. I'm banking my integrity, my own personal sense of integrity, on that statement."

"It's a cycle of overhead," said Jonathan Katz, the Associated Press reporter in Haiti at the time of the earthquake who tracked post-disaster spending for his book, *The Big Truck That Went By*. "It was always going to be the American Red Cross taking a 9 percent cut, re-granting to another group, which would take out their cut." Given the results produced by the Red Cross' projects in Haiti, Jean-Max Bellerive, the former prime minister of Haiti, said he has a hard time fathoming what has happened to donors' money. "Five hundred million dollars in Haiti is a lot of money," he said. "I'm not a big mathematician, but I can make some additions. I know more or less the cost of things. Unless you don't pay for the gasoline the same price I was paying, unless you pay people 20 times what I was paying them, unless the cost of the house you built was five times the cost I was paying, it doesn't add up for me."

Indeed, the organization was not able to pull off the project as had been originally hoped, but had it purposely withheld funds in doing so? The Red Cross responded by saying that competing land claims and other setbacks meant that building new permanent homes, which was the stated goal of the project, wasn't the most efficient and effective way of helping displaced residents. The organization instead focused on providing emergency shelter and transitional homes to meet immediate needs. It also explained that of the $488 million raised for its work in Haiti, $145 million went to health, cholera prevention, and water and sanitation services. While it appears the Red Cross did not live up to public expectations, the over-the-top media coverage painted the organization as an inept swindler.

Nonprofits are especially vulnerable to accusations of failure, fraud or deception. One of the biggest factors predisposing the public to mistrust nonprofits and their staff is the norm of self-interest. The idea that individuals act to increase their own utility is deeply ingrained in the popular dialogue around economics, evolution and social policy. When nonprofits are not entirely transparent, people are apt to think that the organizations are spending the money on themselves and not the causes they are built to advance.

In "The Norm of Self-Interest," Stanford psychology professor Dale T. Miller explains that the public not only sees self-interest as the go-to explanation for behavior, but also a directive by which people *should* live. However, more current research indicates that, in reality, self-interest is only weakly linked to attitudes on social issues such as racial integration. But, the idea that self-interest does (and should) direct action persists; studies suggest that our self-interested nature leads people to feel uncomfortable taking a stand for a cause that doesn't directly affect them. A series of experiments on how the public perceives volunteers found that "the expectation that others will act in self-interested ways can lead observers…to respond with greater negativity toward supporters of a cause who do not have a victimhood experience that connects them to the cause." Nonprofit staff who often work on causes that don't directly affect them can appear as if they are breaking this fundamental social norm. This breeds discomfort and suspicion and leads to questions like, "What are they getting out of this?"

I myself have bought into this norm of self-interest. The organization for which I volunteer, DC SCORES, serves to provide after-school programming to urban children in public schools that lack the resources to provide such programming themselves. The organization does this through after-school soccer leagues and poetry or service-learning classes. I come from a relatively privileged background and always had access to after-school services. I played soccer after school all the way from sixth to 12th grade at no additional cost. Sometimes, I feel a disconnect with my work and feel self-conscious that I do not possess the necessary insights to truly help the organization. For instance, I do not have the same experience or insights as does one of my coworkers who actually went through the program during her time in elementary and middle school. In this way, the norm of self-interest affects me as a volunteer.

Another factor that leads people to criticize nonprofits is a predisposition to label them as "do-gooders" or those who break a social norm in the name of morality. A study on the documented hostility toward vegetarians revealed that when someone acts differently from the norm and attributes it to morality, others assume that the actor is negatively judging them. People assume that the "do-gooder" is questioning their morality. Similarly, when the general public considers someone who has devoted their career to charitable work, they assume these professionals feel morally superior. Portraying nonprofit staff as corrupt or greedy cuts them down to size and mitigates the moral threat.

Allegations of executive greed and excessive compensation crop up frequently as a result of this drive, but an investigation from one of the sector's foremost watchdogs reveals that such cases are rare. Charity Navigator's 2014 Charity CEO Compensation Study gathered data from 3,927 nonprofits. Of these, only 12 offered compensation packages over $1 million to their top executive. That's 0.31 percent. Furthermore, all of these seven-figure packages were collected by CEOs of large organizations with more than $13.5 million in revenue.

With that said, millennials' skepticism toward nonprofit organizations is not unfounded, and calls for transparency are sometimes necessary. For instance, the 2015 Cancer Fund of America investigation was one of the largest charity fraud cases ever. At the center of the operation was James T. Reynolds Sr., who founded the organization in 1987. Over decades, he created three more cancer-focused charitable organizations. In its complaint, the Federal Trade Commission called all four of the cancer groups "sham charities," charging the organizations with deceiving donors and misusing millions of dollars in donations, including putting money toward personal expenses like car washes and college tuition, from 2008 to 2012. There were subscriptions to dating websites, meals at Hooters and purchases at Victoria's Secret—not to mention Jet Ski joy rides and couples' cruises to the Caribbean, all paid for by the more than $200 million in donations for cancer patients.

"Some charities use donations to send children with cancer to Disney World," said Mark Hammond, secretary of state for South Carolina, whose office joined the investigation of the groups in 2012. "In this case, the Children's Cancer Fund of America used donations to send themselves to Disney World." Indeed, the FTC complaint noted that the charities spent less than 3 percent of donations on cancer patients. Hammond said that the revelations were a reminder: "Be vigilant when giving to charity."

There exists in the public sphere an inherent distrust of nonprofit organizations. This is occurring because nonprofit organizations missed out on the technology revolution. Without the additional funds for investment, their internal systems for data tracking became obsolete. Unable to directly link donations to cash outlays or track impact created to show value added, the public jumps to the conclusion that the organizations are taking the money for themselves.

Several systems have come to market that can help nonprofits track their funding and spending to better converse with the public about their costs and how they relate to impact. The Internet of Things has made it increasingly easy for organizations to capture data in innovative ways and from new locations. Nonprofit staff sometimes lack the training to deal with the large amounts of data necessary to be successful today; artificial intelligence processing can make that data more accessible to staff to better inform their decisions and free up time.

Nonprofit organizations are a big and easy target for bad press. The public is trained to distrust nonprofits by the norm of self-interest and by the moral threat of do-gooders. New technologies available today can help to create trust between the two groups and repair relationships and images.

CHAPTER 3

OLD DOG, OLD TRICKS

THE PROBLEM WITH CHARITY WATCHDOGS

"This was a crime born out of entitlement and greed committed to ensure a lifestyle that was beyond their means," U.S. District Judge Timothy Corrigan said, according to the Florida Times-Union. "Just think of the good that could have been done with that money if it would have been used for its intended purpose."

In July of 2016, U.S. Rep. Corrine Brown of Florida and her chief of staff were charged with multiple counts of fraud and other federal offenses in a grand jury indictment after a federal investigation found ties between the congresswoman and a fraudulent charity. The indictment came after an investigation into the charity One Door for Education Foundation Inc., which federal prosecutors say was purported to give scholarships to poor students but instead filled the coffers of Brown and her associates.

The 12-term congresswoman, one of the first black federal representatives in Florida since the 1800s, raised more than $800,000 for the One Door for Education group, which she falsely claimed was a charity raising money for kids. "Brown, Simmons, and Wiley used Brown's official positions as a member of Congress to solicit contributions to One Door for Education and to induce individuals and entities to make donations…based on false and fraudulent representation that the funds would be used for charitable purposes," read the indictment.

Court documents outline allegations that Brown and Simmons took money from the foundation, made cash deposits into their personal bank accounts and used the money to pay for a bevy of personal items—including $5,000 for a magazine cover featuring Brown, nearly $3,000 for a 2013 Miami Beach vacation taken by Wiley and Simmons and $2,643 for repair work on Brown's personal car.

According to the indictment, $200,000 in One Door for Education funds were also used to pay for events either hosted by Brown or held in her honor, including the use of luxury boxes during a Beyoncé concert in Washington, D.C., and an NFL game between the Washington Redskins and Jacksonville Jaguars.

Charity fraud is real and has been a problem in society for a while. It first became a public issue when, in April 1918, *The New York Times* published a story of charity fraud committed by Secretary of the Cripples' Welfare Society George W. Ryder. Ryder pleaded guilty to using mail fraud to use the donations for his personal gain.

About this time, people started clamoring for a better way to know where their donation was going. Some turned to a new type of organization: the charity watchdog. Since then, these organizations have become rather prevalent. Charity watchdogs are helpful because they provide information to help donors avoid fraudulent organizations. However, one problem with this kind of organization is its emphasis on the formulas that rate the financial efficiency of nonprofit organizations. These formulas are heavily influenced by overhead spending rates and will rate an organization poorly if it spends a large amount of its donations on overhead. These calculations can catch criminals spending funds on lavish items or personal wants, but can inadvertently hurt organizations that are functioning properly while investing in technology or other resources.

However, charity watchdogs are still key to protecting the donor. This fact became evident recently in the wake of an extremely serious hurricane season. In one season, we saw hurricanes Harvey, Irma and Maria nail the Gulf Coast and Caribbean.

Hurricane Harvey seemed to spin up in an instant before hitting land on Aug. 26, only to come to rest for days over southeast Texas and southwest Louisiana. A mind-boggling 19 trillion gallons of rain fell in that storm, which triggered unprecedented flooding. Texas Gov. Greg Abbott estimates Harvey will cost the state up to $180 billion—more than epic Hurricane Katrina of 2005. Thousands of water rescues occurred in the Houston metro area as many homes and businesses were swamped by floodwaters.

But, as Harvey's floodwaters were beginning to recede in Houston and the devastating storm was finally loosening its grip on the Gulf Coast, many dangers and hardships still laid in wait for drenched residents in Texas and Louisiana: charity scams. Targeting both Harvey victims and those looking to donate to relief efforts, scam artists tried to use the storm and people's sense of charity to swindle thousands of dollars from unwitting targets.

Americans across the country raced to donate millions of dollars to charities providing relief efforts to victims of Harvey.

Unfortunately, it should come as no surprise that criminals looking to make a quick buck preyed on those with a benevolent heart. There were numerous reports of people receiving phone calls, text messages, emails or posts on their social media accounts that asked for money for Harvey relief efforts.

However, a number of legitimate organizations were also trying to help to collect money for Harvey victims. These nonprofits included the American Red Cross, Direct Relief and Catholic Charities. Without a thorough knowledge of the nonprofit arena, it proved difficult for people to determine which charities were real and which were a scam.

This was where Charity Navigator, a charity watchdog organization, stepped in. The organization released statements warning the public about charity scams and gave them guidelines to avoid such deception. Charity Navigator even compiled a list of highly rated organizations responding in the aftermath of the storm and providing assistance to the people and communities affected by it. The list allowed donors to feel comfortable knowing that their donation would help someone who needed it. Charity Navigator then broke down the list and created categories of charities so that the donor would feel more comfortable and more connected to a cause they really cared about. Through the list, a donor could find charities providing general disaster relief in the wake of Hurricane Harvey, medical services and supplies to those impacted by

Hurricane Harvey, basic necessities and education to children impacted by Hurricane Harvey, or financial assistance to individuals and nonprofits impacted by Hurricane Harvey. The security and depth of choice provided by this organization makes it easier for donors and nonprofits to respond to disasters and serve people in need.

However, let's not forget that most of these charity watchdogs use formulas that actively discourage overhead spending on necessary items such as the technology that can help nonprofits bring social impact into the 21st century. The outdated perception that nonprofits should spend less than 25 percent of operating revenue on overhead has been dragged into the present day by the fear of a low rating from an influential watchdog.

It is no secret how most of these watchdogs perform their calculations. Most even outline their basic formula on their website. They tell donors exactly how they rate organizations on a 5-star scale or grade them A-F.

Let's take a look at CharityWatch, a watchdog organization that has been operating for over 25 years. The organization says that it performs "in-depth evaluations of complex charity financial reporting, including audited financial statements, tax forms, annual reports, state filings, and other documents." For CharityWatch, this involves pulling out two numbers—program percentage and cost—to raise $100. The group average the two results on its scale then assigns the charity a final efficiency rating in the form of a letter grade ranging from A+ to F.

Program percentage reflects the proportion of total expenses a charity spent on its programs in the year analyzed. For example, an organization with a program percentage of 80 percent means that the charity spent 80 percent of its expenses on charitable programs. The remaining 20 percent was spent on overhead. The other metric measures how much it cost the charity to bring in each $100 of cash donations from the public in the year analyzed. For example, a Cost to Raise $100 of $20 means that the charity spent $20 on fundraising for each $100 of cash donations it received.

Having looked at CharityWatch's scale, an organization with overhead spending of 25 percent, which is healthy but not enough in the technology revolution, can receive a grade no higher than a B+. If the organization struggles to capture donations efficiently, its rating will doubly be pulled down.

These rigid regulations of overhead spending rates have starved the nonprofit sector's ability to invest in key innovations of technology. When organizations have such little free funds for investing, technology seems like an unknown, risky investment. As a result, nonprofits are not functioning on the same level as corporations of similar sizes within the private sector. They are not able to deliver the high-quality impact that they otherwise could have created through innovation.

But there is one saving grace for CharityWatch. The organization has analysts go back through an in-depth analysis of financial information after initial numbers have been pulled. These analysts make certain adjustments to figures reported by a charity in its tax filing and/or its audited financial statements to better reflect to donors how efficiently a charity is spending their donations. Thats right; this watchdog actually takes the time to look at investments and track their impact on a program.

For an example of a nonprofit that required additional scrutiny to compile accurate information about its spending, CharityWatch CEO Daniel Borochoff cites the Intrepid Fallen Heroes Fund, which provides services to severely injured military personnel, spending the vast majority of the funds it receives on the construction of research, diagnosis, treatment and medical facilities. Due to accounting rules, the millions of dollars the charity spends on constructing these facilities, typically over a multi-year period, are not reported by the charity as a program expense in the year the funds are spent on construction. As a result, many watchdog organizations give this nonprofit low ratings because the expense of building the hospital cannot be placed under program costs; instead, it must be filed as capital outlay until the hospital is finished.

CharityWatch "understands that while these accounting rules are appropriate for audit and other financial reporting, taking them at face value when computing financial efficiency percentages for any single reporting year would produce volatile results that are not reflective of how efficiently or inefficiently this charity is operating." In the end, the organization gives the Intrepid Fallen Heroes Fund an A rating.

It will be increasingly important for watchdogs to operate on a similar basis as CharityWatch. Simply pulling overhead spending percentages from financial reports will not properly reflect the effectiveness of an organization as it makes an investment in vital technology. Going forward, watchdog organizations need to find a way to track investment in nonprogram costs and the actual impact on program effectiveness that these investments cause. For investments in recruitment or new office materials, for example, this process may be difficult. But technological investment is likely to run into fewer barriers as many technological tools are inherently transparent and provide tracking data automatically.

CharityWatch has analysts bore over financial data, and then has them revisit the same data to make adjustments. Instead, watchdogs and nonprofit organizations could benefit from increased communication. A nonprofit employee could more easily verbalize a connection between investment in technology and the indirect impact it has on program than financial reports can display with charts and figures. Watchdogs are a necessary protector of the public in our exploitative world, but they need to conduct more thorough analyses and focus less on overhead spending rates. The social impact sector as a whole needs to more properly discuss the link between technology and program effectiveness.

CHAPTER 4

GOING BIGGER

STRATEGIC MERGERS AND ACQUISITIONS

"M&A is vital to every industry—it's how companies evolve to better meet the needs of customers cost-effectively. Why should nonprofits, with deep social and environmental impact goals, be any different? If anything, our sector needs more combinations and spin-offs, in order to build more dynamic and effective organizations," says Leila Janah, founder of technology-driven nonprofit Samasource. While long-established nonprofits could theoretically build many technological capabilities in-house, buying through acquisition might be faster, cheaper and less of a headache.

Mergers and acquisitions are underutilized business strategies that could drive easier and more effective adoption of technology within the nonprofit sector. Established nonprofits struggle with innovation, technology and design, but often have scale and credibility. By contrast, nonprofit tech startups excel at innovation, technology and design, but often have limited scale and credibility. The solution, therefore, should be obvious: Traditional nonprofits and startups should join forces to marry old and new assets and talents.

However, M&A in the sector is not unheard of; a Bridgespan report studied 3,300 nonprofit M&A deals across four states over an 11-year period. It found that nonprofit mergers often come about through default due to financial distress or leadership vacuums. Relatively few nonprofits are using M&A strategically: as a way to strengthen organizations' effectiveness, spread best practices, expand reach, and to do all of this more cost-effectively.

Over the past decade, technology-driven nonprofits like Charity Water and Samasource have been on the rise, having captivated mainstream and nonprofit media. A bit of good news for those interested in acquisition: The number of tech nonprofits worldwide is reaching record highs, according to Shannon Farley, the co-founder of the nonprofit accelerator Fast Forward. While no organization is perfect and ripe for acquisition, nonprofit startups have figured out what many traditional nonprofits struggle with; their captivating websites, innovative use of technology and digital outreach serve as a siren song to the next generation of donors.

In 2013, United Cerebral Palsy joined with Seguin Services, creating UCP Seguin Chicago. "Looking back, it's clear that the move was a good one; the combined organization has grown significantly," remarks Donald Haider, who has taught for 43 years and served as director of the Center for Nonprofit Management at the Kellogg School of Management. "The success of the UCP and Seguin merger is all the more remarkable because the organization operates in Illinois—a state where chronic funding delays has forced other disability providers to shut their doors. It took a comprehensive, deliberate, and particularly thoughtful approach to make this merger succeed." One important fact to consider is that the two organizations had been collaborating on projects for five years, and the study on nonprofit M&A had revealed that in 80 percent of success cases, a prior collaboration existed between the merging organizations. The merger process began for UCP when its CEO at the time announced his retirement. Rather than seeking a replacement, he and his board recognized that greater mission and organization sustainability could be generated through a strategic merger with Seguin.

The merger was also successful because of similarities in mission and values. The two organizations shared common values and a mission of service to the disabled; UCP and Seguin operated separately for more than 60 years in the field of disability services, with offerings including residential housing, in-home services, foster care, consulting and income-generating enterprises. The key to success for these two organizations was not only their similarity in mission, but differences in their programs, services and fundraising. UCP promoted independence for children and adults through a multistate enterprise called Infinitec: access to information, training, and equipment such as computers. Seguin Industries was a pioneer in integrated community living in group homes and through in-home support services. UCP had key industry advantages in technology, and Seguin had key advantages in facilities.

Their combined success was further possible due to the financial strength of each organization individually. UCP and Seguin were $9 million and $27 million organizations respectively; the costs of their respective programs and overhead were compared and contrasted. UCP had been celebrated in a *Chicago Magazine* article featuring local charities with the lowest overhead costs. Both also had high ratings from charitable watchdog organizations. "We were two healthy organizations, both at the right time in their histories when they could take on a merger partner," says Paul Dulle, a leading staff member at UCP. "Whether they merged into us or we merged into them was not the issue. the point is that we put our resources together and created something better."

Haider says, "While the complementary structure of these two organizations provided logic for the merger, the key to the merger success was trust." In fact, Dulle told the study group, "Trust overcomes fear, which is the biggest impediment to change, and to a merger." To remove merger fear from the onset, organization leaders assured staff that, should merger talks proceed further, no one would lose their job, benefits, or current compensation. The organizations were able to ensure this, in part, because they were both financially strong. Trust built at all levels of the two organizations enabled the merger process to work. Integration of the two organizations began before the formal merger and developed smoothly thereafter.

The merger has been successful on several fronts so far. Three years following the merger, the organization's revenues exceeded $43 million, a 14 percent increase. Combined net assets for the two organizations over the period were $23 million a significant strengthening of their balance sheets and cash reserves. They were also able to increase funding to grow all programs: children's foster care grew more than 50 percent, residential care grew 13 percent, home-based care doubled in size, day services were increased by 60 percent, and work services grew by 22 percent.

A recent study, produced by a partnership between Northwestern University's Kellogg School of Management, Mission and Strategy Consulting and eight Chicago foundations, revealed that nonprofit mergers hold great promise. Having analyzed 25 nonprofit mergers that occurred in the Chicago area between 2004 and 2014, including uncompleted and dissolved mergers, the study found that in 88 percent of the cases that were studied, both the acquired and the acquiring nonprofits reported that their organization was better off after the merger, with "better" being defined in terms of achieving organizational goals and increasing collective impact.

Yet, nonprofit consultant Thomas McLaughlin noted in his book *Nonprofit Mergers and Alliances*, "To some in the nonprofit field, the idea of mergers is scandalous and distasteful." Haider reiterates that sentiment adding that, "Because as a sector, we still don't know much about nonprofit mergers. Even the *idea* of two nonprofits merging still seems alien—or worse—to many people in the field." To understand why mergers may be more common in the private sector, it is helpful to consider some of the differences between for-profit and nonprofit organizations.

Nonprofit mergers tend to fail as a result of a few organizational constraints. When these merging ventures are executed successfully, it is often because both organizations were financially healthy. But traditionally, nonprofit M&A occurs in response to the financial distress of one member. While two nonprofits merging may expand their service area, improve their operations, or increase their efficiency, because of organizational structure and the nonprofit label they are unlikely to make more money by doing so. Nonprofit organizations cannot simply acquire another nonprofit by purchasing the controlling share of stock because there are no shareholders. Similarly, a nonprofit cannot acquire another nonprofit and then boost revenue by selling off the programs that it considers unprofitable.

Another barrier to nonprofit M&A is that the staff and board are committed to the organization's independent mission and legacy. Overwhelmingly, people create and work for nonprofits that they are deeply passionate about; they are serious about making a difference for a specific cause and may even be personally affected by it. The most successful mergers are mission-driven, but it can still be difficult for certain staff or board members to let go of their specific mission and verbiage in M&A. In addition, staff and board members fear losing their jobs in a new organization that won't need two of a certain position, such as executive director. As mentioned before, financial constraints may make it difficult for one organization to satiate the payroll of two.

Nonprofit M&A is not doomed to fail, however; there are certainly ways to avoid or overcome these obstacles. In this same Kellogg School of Management study, the researchers uncovered several well-planned and strategically anchored mergers that produced greater growth and more services.

"From an external industry and market perspective, success turned on the ability of these organizations to understand each other's competencies and figure out how combining those competencies would enhance their competitive position."

There are a few reasons why acquisitions of nonprofit startups should be particularly attractive to legacy organizations. First of all, founders of these startups, many of them recent graduates, have grown up with technology and design and have an impressive understanding of the space. Tools like WordPress, MailChimp, Classy, Salesforce, Klout, and G Suite make it easy for nonprofit entrepreneurs to quickly establish and manage a digital brand on a budget without backend IT, design or communications support. For example, a Twitter hashtag campaign can be set up with affordable, user-friendly technology, while only requiring a small team of tech savvy employees.

In addition, these millennials often have a better grasp on data collection software and more experience with data-driven decisions than do their older counterparts. With such little capital and no margin for error, nonprofit startups have to experiment to see what sticks and learn quickly. That often means using Google Analytics, A/B testing, focus groups and other data-driven methods to ensure that the organization is getting the most out of its website, digital advertising and content marketing, useful still to large legacy organizations.

As we will discuss later, an increasing number of the nonprofit startups that millennials create function as social enterprises rather than as traditional nonprofits. Social enterprises are in the unique position in which a significant portion of their revenue is unrestrained and can be reinvested in innovation and technology. Millennial startups that have developed exciting digital tools with the purpose of creating social change should be extremely attractive targets for acquisition in the eyes of traditional and legacy nonprofit organizations.

In my conversation with Shannon Farley, co-founder of FastForward, a nonprofit startup accelerator program, she highlighted WattTime as an example an M&A success story. Rocky Mountain Institute, founded in 1982 to transform global energy use to create a clean, prosperous, and secure low-carbon future, acquired and incorporated WattTime as a subsidiary organization, "supporting its growth to empower more customers to choose clean energy and reduce their carbon footprint cost-effectively with automated emissions reduction (AER) technology at an unprecedented scale."

WattTime produces software that can automatically detect the actual emissions impact when people and companies use energy, both in real time and ahead of time. The software can be installed in any internet-connected device to harness the power of electric grid data and predictive analytics to automatically pull power from the grid at times when energy sources are the cleanest, with no effect on the device or end user. "We created WattTime to give people a new sort of freedom: to choose the power they consume," said Gavin McCormick, WattTime co-founder and executive director.

Imagine you need to vacuum your room. You've got a vacuum that needs to be plugged into the wall. What WattTime can allow you to do is check what power source that electricity is coming from. You open up an app on your phone and you see that the electricity right now is being generated by burning fossil fuels. Wait five minutes. Electricity is now being generated by solar panels or wind turbines; vacuum away, my friend.

"To do this, our organization does two things. We provide the most accurate and actionable information possible so any person, or company, can see their own impact; and we write software that makes it automatic and utterly effortless to implement their choice at the push of a button. Today, our partnership with RMI allows us to maintain this ambitious pursuit and amplify our impact even further."

The partnership greatly benefits WattTime; the organization immediately increases its reach and impact to encompass all of RMI's partner organizations, not just WattTime's own early-adopters. RMI and WattTime expect the technology to be more broadly used in an effort to accelerate corporate sustainability efforts, improve the profitability of distributed energy resource companies and retail energy providers by lowering customer acquisition costs, and improve the way that carbon emissions are measured worldwide.

Rocky Mountain Institute benefits as well; the legacy organization could not have reasonably created the same product in-house with the resources used to acquire the startup. Now that it has the product, the organization can better achieve its mission to accelerate the adoption of market-based solutions that cost-effectively shift from fossil fuels to efficiency and renewables. "RMI has a strong history of scaling disruptive, market-based solutions that can help us win the battle against climate change, and WattTime absolutely fits these criteria," said Jules Kortenhorst, RMI chief executive officer. "Together, WattTime and RMI can pioneer a new way to measure carbon and empower customers to reduce emissions cost-effectively, realizing long-term benefits for the grid, customers, manufacturers, and utilities while immediately offering economic and environmental benefits to corporations and people."

Millennials understand technology and possess the ability to find unique and innovative ways to use these new tools to drive social change. Members of this generation are starting their own nonprofit organizations and social enterprises and are trying to scale their impact. Larger nonprofits, which need this technology to stay relevant and effective in the new age, should be on the lookout for potential partners or targets that could make a real change.

PART 2

THE MILLENNIAL INFLUENCE

CHAPTER 5

THE MILLENNIAL'S NONPROFIT

―

A SOCIAL ENTERPRISE

―

On December 26th, 2013, an 18-month-old child from a remote community in the Guinean rainforest fell ill and died tragically of cholera-like symptoms. Within weeks, several of his family members had succumbed to the same fate. Local Public Health officials had no idea that this would become the largest Ebola epidemic in recorded history. Having started as a local outbreak in a remote community, Ebola quickly overwhelmed the region's fragile health systems and claimed the lives of more than 11,300 people across Guinea, Liberia and Sierra Leone.

I remember the Ebola outbreak. Flights were canceled; it was mass panic. Not long after the second nurse to contract Ebola was identified, the public learned that she had flown on a commercial flight after being exposed to the disease. It was all over the news. So many health care workers clad head to toe in yellow hazmat suits were risking their lives to help these extremely sick people. Who were they? Where did they come from?

In the aftermath of the Ebola outbreak, Last Mile Health supported the government of Liberia in designing a nationwide community health workforce initiative called the National Community Health Assistant Program. Liberia had emerged from more than a decade of civil war in 2003, and after years of violence, the country's health infrastructure was devastated. Only 50 doctors remained to treat a population of more than 4 million people. A co-founder of the organization that would become Last Mile Health remembers, "Almost immediately, our growing team realized that the greatest needs were at Liberia's last mile, where people in remote communities lacked access to healthcare due to distance and poverty."

Last Mile Health assisted the government of Liberia to train and equip community health workers and health facility staff across Liberia's southeastern region to respond to the epidemic and to provide lifesaving routine health services while remaining safe from infection. The social enterprise also trained hundreds of community mobilizers to prevent and contain the spread of Ebola. They partnered with Direct Relief, a nonprofit humanitarian aid organization, to distribute 22 tons of personal protective equipment, like gloves and goggles.

Hold up. What actually is a social enterprise? Social enterprises can be for-profit or nonprofit, but are considered a subsection of the nonprofit sector in most literature. Nonprofit social enterprises are those entities that sell merchandise, such as articles made by artisans, that help provide an economic path out of poverty. For-profit businesses are considered social enterprises when they are not only using financial profits as a measurement of success, but also social impact. However, what solidifies social enterprises within the category of nonprofit organizations is that their social mission is as core to their success as any potential profit. These organizations really do value their mission and the impact they have on beneficiaries.

The millennial generation—ages 16 to 29—has driven significant growth in social enterprises over the last decade or more, reshaping the nonprofit sector and designing many charitable organizations that are starting to look more and more like for-profit entities. A social enterprise applies commercial strategies to maximize impact in humanitarian efforts and environmental well-being.

"Governments are not equipped to solve all of the world's problems—nor should they be—and are looking for innovative solutions from the private sector. Social entrepreneurs will play a vital role," says Siri Terjesen, co-author of a special report on social entrepreneurship for the Global Entrepreneurship Monitor. This has contributed to the growing number nonprofit organizations, and more currently, social enterprises. "Social and environmental problems are ubiquitous in all economies. Hence, politicians, business leaders, and members of society are increasingly calling for endeavours that focus on social and environmental objectives—and entrepreneurs are responding," says Mike Herrington, executive director of the Global Entrepreneurship Monitor.

What I find exciting about social enterprises is the fact that they have different revenue streams than do traditional nonprofits. Instead of having vital funds tied up to specific programs or positions, social enterprises have actual sales revenue that they can spend or reinvest as a for-profit company would. The way that I see it, social enterprises are just nonprofit organizations with the ability to invest in technology, which is very exciting.

My favorite example of a social enterprise is Moms Avenue. Evelina Bajorune founded the social enterprise to encourage women, and moms in particular, to embrace the growth of blockchain technologies and capitalize on advantages presented by cryptocurrency markets. The cryptocurrency space suffers from diversity issues. Surveys indicate that more than 90 percent of Bitcoin users are male. Bajorune also believes strongly in empowering women to start their own small businesses, so another part of the mission is to provide risk free capital to mothers who are trying to establish themselves as social entrepreneurs.

An experienced project manager at Barclays Group Operations Lithuania and mother of one, Bajorune developed Moms Avenue. Moms Avenue is a cryptocurrency market that exists on the Ethereum ecosystem. Ethereum is an open software platform based on blockchain technology; developers and nonprofit organizations cam build and deploy decentralized blockchain-based applications on this platform. The Moms Avenue application runs on smart contracts, a reward system enabled by the blockchain technology.

Bajorune saw the an opportunity to create a community where mothers from around the world who lack sufficient resources could improve their lives and spark community development through the growth of their own small businesses. Bajorune decided to emulate Etsy, a New York-based mobile marketplace where users sell unique handmade goods. On the topic of Etsy, she says, "This platform is going to be useful not only for moms who aim to start their own businesses but also to anyone who would like to buy unique handcrafted goods. Etsy was created to sell handmade or vintage items, but now it has become a place for mass production and less than top-quality stuff. Last year consumers spent $34 billion, on general crafts, fine arts, jewelry and bead crafts in the U.S. Etsy's annual gross merchandise sales grew to $2.39 billion, and its number of active sellers reached 1.56 million. Moms Avenue will be the innovative solution to enter into this market ensuring high-quality content driven by its community."

Moms Avenue utilizes a commercial business practice referred to as a "freemium" service to more effectively grow the value added to stakeholders, but more importantly, the community of mothers. Freemium services are pricing models in which the basic or core services are provided for free, but additional services are available for purchase. Other commercial strategies include payment of dividends to certain external shareholders that may request or require such an incentive.

One popular commercial example of a freemium service is Pandora Radio. The company gives away the base music streaming service for free, but then charges a subscription fee for premium levels of the product. Under the freemium strategy, the basic service is available for everyone at no cost, but with strict limitations in bandwidth and ads that pop up between songs, which results in a lower quality listening experience. Pandora charges $36 for a yearly subscription of the premium service.

Pandora has historically generated most of its revenue from the ads it can sell to target the free users. However, the premium membership fees boost its total revenue and give it extra capital to reinvest. For the fiscal year 2016, membership fees accounted for over 16 percent of Pandora's total revenue. Imagine if a nonprofit could increase its funding by 16 percent and reinvest that into innovating and streamlining its value or support delivery services with technology. This is why we see the turn to social enterprise structures.

In a report led by Neils Bosma, a professor at Utrecht University School of Economics, adding information about trends in social enterprise, he says, "Social entrepreneurship is often associated with young change-makers who are idealistic in nature." In fact, over the course of the last decade, Ivy League schools and top-ranked business programs have shown an increased interest in social entrepreneurship. The number of social entrepreneurship courses offered at top MBA programs across the United States increased by 110 percent between 2003 and 2009. At one school in particular, Harvard University, the number of students enrolled in the Social Enterprise Career Program has almost doubled since 2006. Members of the faculty and student body at Stanford have similarly become leaders in cutting-edge research in the social impact sector; the Stanford Social Innovation Review is an extremely popular publication. These findings complement our established understanding of millennials and their view toward philanthropy and the world.

Alan Mahon is a social entrepreneur based in Edinburgh who has a global impact. Previously a business development manager at Social Bite, a chain of sandwich shops that focuses on helping homeless people, Mahon is a co-founder of Brewgooder, a craft beer company that reinvests 100 percent of its profits toward clean water projects in developing countries. "If you don't have a sustainable way of tackling a problem, then your impact will be short term," he says. "The beauty of what we're doing is that there is an inherent commerciality—that is the driver—but that gives us our point of difference and a platform to do something philanthropic and socially beneficial. I work to build a scalable business, but we want to make a difference out of what comes out of it. Can I work for the benefit of people I may never see? Of course I can."

Social entrepreneurship is the new American dream. Growing emphasis on social good in society is empowering millennials to balance their career goals with karma. There is a clear tendency among students and recent graduates to take pay cuts to work for a company that reflects their values; an article by Business Civic Leadership Center showed that 65 percent of university students expect to make a difference in future jobs and 58 percent would agree to a 15 percent pay cut to do so.

Moms Avenue aims to reduce the costs of entry for mothers. Average market entry costs for small-to-medium sized businesses tally to $30,000; even for a micro-business, cost of entry remains steep at $3,000. It costs nothing to join the community on Mom's avenue, participants just need to cover the costs of the raw materials and inputs for their goods or services. Evelin clarifies the value proposition to participants in saying, "The solution Moms Avenue is proposing will allow you to turn your hobby into a successful and profitable business and not risk anything at all. On the contrary, it will provide a possibility to receive the support and guidance from experienced entrepreneurs, find partners for your business, share ideas, get most of the benefit from vibrant and robust community and get rewarded."

As mentioned before, the platform operates on smart contracts. That means when customers in the marketplace verify receipt of goods, and only then do the participants receive payment. M.O.M. tokens are the base currency on the blockchain. Mothers and their businesses invest zero dollars but still have the chance to grow a token wallet. Participants can use these tokens to purchase goods and services from others on the network.

Mothers who have or have built up sufficient resources can also use these tokens to purchase the additional freemium services and products from Moms Avenue that can help to better develop and expand their business. These services include a job board to find potential collaborators or employees, specially developed advertising campaigns to better reach customers, and a 'business kick-off tool' that helps these women find investors to give their organization a boost.

Vincentas Vitkauskas who works on the Business Development team at Moms Avenue says, "Our performance will be evaluated by the new ventures created and the value established for the community." This marketplace really does have an aim to create change in the community and bring greater opportunity to women and mothers. The fact that beneficiaries have to pay for some services and that the organization pays some dividends does not diminish the value of its mission; Moms Avenue still has the goals of a nonprofit organization. The system simply uses the freemium business model to be more competitive and effective in delivering services by providing itself back-up funding or extra resources to invest in innovation and growth.

The number of social enterprise organizations like Moms Avenue is climbing as a result of millennial preferences and values. These organizations represent new revenue streams within the social impact sector. Social entrepreneurs essentially create nonprofits with healthy amounts of funding for innovation, technology and ultimately, growth.

Millennials are rapidly becoming the largest population within the workforce. Their values demand a new work-life balance, one that includes giving back and creating impact. This is why we see the growth in the sector.

Most traditional nonprofits missed the boat during the technology revolution. The benefits that new and emerging technologies offer to nonprofit organizations in changing the world are countless. But, the overhead simply can't be sacrificed. That is the beauty of the social enterprise: It relies significantly less on foundations and grants, it makes the call on investment. When enterprising millennials—born and raised in the era of technology—finally get their hands on the funds they need to change the world, exciting things happen.

CHAPTER 6

HITCH A RIDE

CORPORATE SOCIAL RESPONSIBILITY AND PARTNERSHIPS

"The President Stole Your Land"

For two days in early December 2017, any person trying to get onto Patagonia's website would get redirected to a black screen displaying the text above. No fleeces, no snow pants; there was no going anywhere without seeing this screen. You had to scroll through the message to reach the shopping section of the website. The message continued in smaller letters: "In an illegal move, the president just reduced the size of Bears Ears and Grand Staircase-Escalante National

Monuments. This is the largest elimination of protected land in American history."

The message was in reference to President Trump's recent executive order reducing the size of two national monuments in Utah by nearly 2 million acres combined. Patagonia's message included illustrations showing what part of the two monuments would no longer be protected and facts about protected lands, noting that "90 percent of U.S. public lands are open to oil and gas leasing and development; only 10 percent are protected for recreation, conservation and wildlife."

But the question remains: Why would the outdoor recreation company risk losing the sales of products on the landing page? Many online shoppers will leave a webpage if they do not see anything that attracts them right away. The answer: the millennial consumer. Millennials care about their values when making purchasing decisions. Shoppers in this generation prefer brands that support a cause.

Patagonia has long been an active participant in the fight to protect the environment. According to the company's website, all the way back in 1986, the company pledged to give 10 percent of its profits to small groups focused on either saving or restoring natural habitats. Private, for-profit companies see the value in associating their brand with that of a nonprofit organization or general cause. As a result, they are willing to invest in charitable causes one way or another.

Nonprofit organizations stand to capitalize on the private sector's campaign for corporate social responsibility. The website urged people to take to social media, using the hashtag #MonumentalMistakes to protest the order. Many Instagram users posted photographs of the two landscapes, circulating the message even further. The added exposure that Patagonia gives to the cause is invaluable. In addition, the company has pledged resources to file a lawsuit against the order.

As for-profit companies spend more and more on developing their social image, nonprofit organizations should look for corporate partnership opportunities to capture significant funding. These corporations can usually make or fundraise extremely large contributions, larger than most individuals can. Nonprofits should target this kind of donor because the size of the donation can help free up other capital resources that the organization can reinvest into vital departments, such as technology.

Patagonia displayed its corporate social responsibility through a basic form of cause marketing, bringing attention to an organization or cause; there are other forms of cause marketing that we will discuss. When private companies make large donations, it is called corporate philanthropy. Private foundation arms actually make the donations for the company. For example, IKEA makes contributions to nonprofit organizations through its charitable arm, the IKEA Foundation.

IKEA is responsible for the first solar plant built in a refugee setting in the world. Funded by the IKEA Foundation's Brighter Lives for Refugees campaign, in January 2017, the solar farm brought renewable power to Jordan's Azraq refugee camp. The solar farm was projected to create an immediate savings of $1.5 million per year and reduce carbon dioxide emissions by 2,370 tons per year. Once the solar plant is upgraded from 2 to 5 megawatts and operating at full capacity, it will increase these savings and continue to reduce carbon dioxide emissions to cover all of Azraq's energy needs. Connected to the national grid, any extra electricity generated will be sent back free of cost, supporting the host community's energy needs.

"The world's first solar farm in a refugee camp signals a paradigm shift in how the humanitarian sector supports displaced populations. UNHCR Jordan will save millions of dollars, while reducing carbon emissions and improving living conditions for some of the world's most vulnerable children and families," said Per Heggenes, CEO of the IKEA Foundation. As the philanthropic arm of INGKA Foundation, which owns the IKEA Group of companies, its mission is to to create substantial and lasting change by funding holistic, long-term programs in some of the world's poorest communities to address children's fundamental needs—home, health, education and a sustainable family income—while helping communities fight and cope with climate change.

In Jordan, where the cost of electricity is high, the solar plant will allow UNHCR, the United Nations Refugee Agency, to provide electricity to Azraq camp residents free of cost, saving money that will be invested in other assistance. The 2-megawatt solar photovoltaic plant will allow UNHCR to provide affordable and sustainable electricity to 20,000 Syrian refugees living in almost 5,000 shelters in Azraq camp, covering the energy needs of the two villages connected to the national grid. Each family can now connect a fridge, a TV and a fan, and have light inside the shelter and charge their phones, which is critical for refugees to keep in contact with their relatives abroad.

The Azraq camp opened its doors in April 2014. Lack of electricity was one of the main challenges its residents faced, making daily activities difficult, such as cooking, washing the clothes, studying or walking safely to the washroom at night, especially for women and children. In 2017, when the IKEA Foundation stepped in with its contribution and introduced electricity, its addressed these challenges and significantly improved the well-being of Azraq residents.

"Today marks a milestone. Lighting up the camp is not only a symbolic achievement; it provides a safer environment for all camp residents, opens up livelihoods opportunities, and gives children the chance to study after dark. Above all, it allows all residents of the camps to lead more dignified lives," said Kelly T. Clements, UNHCR deputy high commissioner. "Once again the partnership between IKEA Foundation and UNHCR has shown how we can embrace new technologies, innovation and humanity while helping refugees."

Private companies focus their efforts on profit; it's all about being in the black. However, these companies still make large donations and coordinate significant efforts on behalf of nonprofit organizations and causes. They make these contributions because there is tried and true data that proves millennials want to purchase products from companies that are socially responsible and actively support causes that they care about. The company expects to profit from this arrangement by selling more products and by enjoying the "halo" effect of being associated with a respected nonprofit or cause. The private sector also knows that millennials now control $2.45 trillion in spending power.

Millennials are 60 percent more likely to engage with brands that discuss social causes, according to Cone Communications. The 2015 Cone Communications Millennial CSR Study found that more than nine in 10 millennials would switch brands to one associated with a cause. In addition, Omnicom Group's Cone Communications also found that 70 percent of surveyed millennials will spend more on brands supporting causes they care about.

It is not very hard to see why corporations are investing time and effort into corporate social responsibility efforts. However, nonprofits should be more aware of opportunities coming from these areas within the corporate sector. Last year, corporations in the United States donated more than $17.77 billion to nonprofit organizations, including arts and cultural organizations, health and human services and educational institutions. Walmart is the largest corporate philanthropist, giving over $300 million annually in cash donations plus over $1 billion in additional in-kind support.

But as I mentioned before, cause marketing can be a strategy corporations use to achieve a positive corporate social image, which is not measured by donation amount. According to cause marketing data compiled by CauseGood, the growth of cause marketing grew from a $120 million industry in 1990 to a more than $2 billion industry in 2016. In fact, a 2010 PRWeek/Barkeley Cause Survey found that 97 percent of marketing executives believe cause marketing is a valid business strategy.

There are a few cause marketing strategies that companies use to drive value for nonprofit organizations. Depending on the way that a nonprofit organization functions, some strategies work more effectively than others. For example, Patagonia's web ads used what is called social or public service marketing programs. There are also product sales promotions wherein a portion of the selling price goes to an organization or cause.

Some millennials actually prefer these cause marketing strategies to corporate philanthropy. According to a 2010 Edelman GoodPurpose Survey, 64 percent of shoppers say simply giving money away isn't enough; they want businesses to integrate social impact directly into their business models, like with buy-one-give-one campaigns. In 2009, Neil Blumenthal, Dave Gilboa, Andy Hunt and Jeff Raider used this cause marketing strategy at a level of perfection, breaking into the U.S. eyewear market. This strategy helped them penetrate this market, of which 90 percent of the market share was held by one company. Today, Warby Parker is estimated to be valued over a $1 billion.

The eyewear company was classified as a B Corps: for-profit companies certified by the nonprofit B Lab to meet rigorous standards of social and environmental performance, accountability and transparency. B Corps is to business what Fair Trade certification is to coffee or USDA Organic certification is to milk. Rather than donating the glasses outright, the company makes cash donations from its sales to VisionSpring, a nonprofit for which Warby Parker founder Neil Blumenthal used to work. "If you're just giving something away, you don't have the market as a mechanism to determine whether or not the consumer really wants your product, whereas when you ask the consumer to pay, you know clearly where that person places value," Jordan Kassalow, VisionSpring's founder, told *Forbes*.

VisionSpring trains low-income men and women to sell glasses in their communities for affordable prices, ensuring that Warby Parker's donations actually meet people's needs and don't displace local businesses. The organization estimates that as many as 90 percent of the world's visually impaired people live in developing countries and 703 million people could have their vision restored simply with a pair of glasses.

Kassalow recalls the moment he decided to found the organization during a trip to Mexico, "On the first day of the trip, we arrived at our site to find 2,000 people in line waiting to have their eyes checked. One of those in line was a 7-year-old boy who was carrying a braille book. The boy's family explained that he was blind but as I started to examine his eyes I soon realized that the boy was just extremely myopic. His prescription was a -20.00D and, incredibly, we were able to fit him with a pair of donated glasses with a -19 prescription." Since its inception, the Warby Parker Buy a Pair, Give a Pair partnership has distributed over 3 million pairs of glasses through VisionSpring.

"As I placed the glasses on the boy's nose, I watched as the blank stare of a blind person transformed into an expression of unadulterated joy—I was witnessing someone seeing his world for the first time." Improved vision really makes an impact individually in a person's life, and also on the world as a whole; VisionSpring estimates that uncorrected vision results in a $202 million loss in the global economy.

Warby Parker's philanthropic efforts were the key in disrupting what was essentially a monopoly. Millennials are rapidly becoming the largest and most powerful consumer group. This generation values corporate social responsibility heavily. As a result, brands are investing billions of dollars in their social image. Corporations and private foundations contribute significantly to the social sector through cause marketing and corporate philanthropy.

Nonprofits can benefit greatly from this private sector eagerness to donate and develop a social image. The Restoration Fund raised over $1.7 million when American Express gave a portion of every purchase through its credit card to the cause. AmEx got its goat too; card use rose 27 percent and new card applications increased 45 percent over the previous year. Nonprofits that have not already developed corporate partnerships should focus their efforts into doing so.

CHAPTER 7

INVESTING IN GOOD

HOW MILLENNIALS SEE IMPACT

The vast majority of children in developing countries aren't dying from unknown diseases or acts of war. They perish because their parents can't find medicine or a trained health care worker in time. Did you know that one-third of all malaria medicines are actually fakes, counterfeits imported mainly from China? It has become a $4 billion industry and another unjust hurdle for those living in poverty to jump through.

Living Goods, a nonprofit organization working to get life-saving health products into the hands of people in need, is often nicknamed the "Avon of Africa" because it trains women to sell products door-to-door. But instead of beauty products, the women sell essential medicines. Women apply to become trained as licensed Community Health Promoters and in turn, they earn an income while caring for their communities. A recent five-year study revealed that having just one CHP in your village reduces child mortality by over 25 percent. This is an incredible achievement. On the back of this data, Living Goods is tirelessly trying to expand as much as possible, operating in Uganda and now in Kenya.

Where do they get the funds to train these people? That is where The Adventure Project's initiative called the Collective comes into play. This movement rides on the back of an extremely effective monthly donation platform. Donors sign up to make a small, automatic monthly contribution and, in doing so, join to create jobs around the globe. The Collective provides people, currently living in extreme poverty, with tools, job training and support to become profitable entrepreneurs.

For example, the Collective helped Grace to become a CHP for Living Goods. Grace became a CHP out of necessity. Her husband recently passed away from a sudden illness, leaving her alone and without income. She lived in a remote village in Uganda and acted through Living Goods to create a pipeline of vital medicines, walking or riding a bike to the local branch to collect more supplies. Armed with over 60 health products, she does not just treat illnesses; CHPs also prevent them by selling bed nets, water filters and vitamin-fortified foods.

Another individual in the village, Ruth, says, "They call her, 'the kind one.'" Her first week on the job, a woman came to Grace's door frazzled and desperate saying, "My children are dying, please help me." All three children had malaria; the mother broke down in tears and pleaded, "Grace, please help, I don't have any money for the medicine right now. Can you please help me?" Grace selflessly lent her the medicine. She was living in poverty as well, and this job selling medicine was her only income, so she would forgo that income if she gave it away. A few days later, the children recovered. The neighbor set out to repay Grace for the money she borrowed. As she went, she exuberantly danced through the streets of the village shouting at every neighbor she passed with arms raised, "Grace saved my children's lives! If you are sick, you need to see Grace! Grace is the kind one."

Grace now cares for over 800 people in her community and has treated over 300 cases of malaria.

The Collective has done an effective job of capturing repeat donors and a steady stream of funds through a monthly donation feature. This is why the group can contribute to great causes. The success of monthly donations is not abnormal; these contributions are fueled by millennials. As of 2015, millennials are the largest generation in the country, as well as in the workplace. As this generation continues to shape the way people work, interact, give, volunteer and make buying decisions, their preferences will ultimately become the norm.

Nonprofits will have to respond and evolve to fit these millennial preferences if they want to capture donations. And there are donors out there that are ripe for the picking; the 2013 Millennial Impact Report revealed that 83 percent of millennial respondents said they gave a gift to a nonprofit organization last year. This generation brings new expectations to charitable giving, and they demand new kinds of information from charitable organizations. Nonprofits can successfully meet these expectations with a few easy, yet key, digital strategies.

Organizations can easily integrate a monthly donation option into their mobile payment processors. Millennials are always online and prefer to donate through the web. Also, millennials prefer to make regular small donations as opposed to large one-time donations. Becoming a monthly donor makes millennials feel more invested in a cause and the growth and impact of the organization.

"The Adventure Project regularly provides stories and pictures of the women and men whose lives have changed because of my simple monthly gift and I love knowing that my donation is having an impact in the lives of others," reads one testimonial for the Collective. It has been successful because it shows monthly donors their impact over time.

Millennials treat their donations as investments in social good, and they want to see a return on their investment. Nonprofits can create graphics on their website that track impact data and communicate that information to potential donors. Most of this data already exists in financial statements or annual reports, but it is key to make it easily accessible on the website so that their millennial donors can access it.

The Collective has not only succeeded because of the monthly donation option, but also because it clearly communicates impact value to potential donors. Returning to the example of Grace the CHP, in the impact report about her, the Collective writes above the donation form "Every $2,000 we raise will train one woman like Grace to care for 800 people in her community. Every $25 will provide health care to 10 people." By tying a real impact to real value, donors can more easily see that return on investment.

Millennials are also avid users of social media, and they bring a social media sensibility to their charitable giving.

Their online identities express who they are and what they care about. They want to share the causes they care about with friends and colleagues. Nonprofit organizations can more easily capture potential donors by making it easy for them to share their donation and impact and to give off that signal to their followers.

A prime example of the success and impact of peer-to-peer fundraising is the ALS Ice Bucket Challenge. The Ice Bucket Challenge was inescapable in 2014, as it spread like a chain letter across Facebook. The fundraising tool had become a meme. Justin Bieber, Lebron James, Oprah Winfrey and Bill Gates were among the endless parade of celebrities who did it, it being dumping a freezing bucket of water on your head and nominating certain friends to do the same.

There was in excess of 2.4 million ice bucket-related videos posted on Facebook, and 28 million people uploaded, commented on or liked ice bucket-related posts. On Instagram, there were 3.7 million videos uploaded with the hashtags #ALSicebucketchallenge and #icebucketchallenge. I remember being tagged by my friend to do the challenge. It was easy to join the movement and I felt driven to become part of something larger. I remember that my mom did the challenge too; that is a funny video. The challenge spread as wildly as it did because the premise involved people reaching out to each other on social media with a simple request: Film yourself getting water dumped over your head or donate money to research on amyotrophic lateral sclerosis, known as Lou Gehrig's disease.

As videos spread across social media and people introduced the cause as a part of their identities, donations poured into the website. Supporters ended up raising upwards of $115 million for the ALS Association over the Summer of 2014. With the millions raised for research from the viral stunt, the ALS Association said it was able to fund research that identified a new gene, NEK1, that contributes to the disease. In reference to the viral peer-to-peer fundraising challenge, lead researcher Philip Wong, a professor at Johns Hopkins, said to the Washington Post, "Without it, we wouldn't have been able to come out with the studies as quickly as we did."

"Global collaboration among scientists, which was really made possible by ALS Ice Bucket Challenge donations, led to this important discovery," said John Landers of the University of Massachusetts, who was one of the lead researchers, in a statement. "It is a prime example of the success that can come from the combined efforts of so many people, all dedicated to finding the causes of ALS. This kind of collaborative study is, more and more, where the field is headed."

There is plenty of research to put this phenomenon into perspective. According to the 2013 Millennial Impact Report, 70 percent of millennials are willing to raise money on behalf of a nonprofit they care about. Around 64 percent have experience peer-to-peer fundraising for walk/run/cycling events, and 45 percent of respondents said that they are not afraid to ask family and friends for money when they feel strongly about a cause. The best way to allow millennials to fundraise on your behalf is to enable social sharing through social media platforms. Millennials are avid users of social media, and they bring a social media sensibility to their charitable giving. One study performed by Artez Interactive found that peer-to-peer campaigns like walkathons generated 15 to 18 percent of their donations through Facebook; 28 percent of the traffic referred to nonprofit fundraising pages came from that platform, with those visitors making a gift 23 percent of the time.

The same Millennial Impact report researched the propensity of the generation to dedicate monthly donations. Millennials, still at the genesis of their professional careers, may lack the direct financial resources to make larger one-time gifts like their older counterparts do. This makes them even more likely to make the monthly investment in an organization: The report indicated that 52 percent of surveyed millennials reported being interested in monthly giving.

This is important information for nonprofits that should be aware of the benefits inherent to receiving a stream of monthly donations. According to Network for Good's donation data, the average recurring donor will give 42 percent more in one year than those who give one-time gifts. The average monthly recurring gift for Network for Good clients is $52, which becomes a $624 donation over the year. A smart monthly giving program will also help an organization reach new segments and convert donors who may otherwise not give. Recurring gifts help donors fit giving into their monthly budgets and allow them to see that being more generous is possible; if donors feel like they can't give enough to make a difference, they may not give at all. Finally, a loyal monthly donor gives an organization a steady stream of money to count on, which in turn, helps nonprofits plan for the future and set aside funds to invest in vital technology.

Attachment to particular organizations or institutions does not drive millennials; they are passionate about specific causes and helping people. That's one reason millennials want nonprofits to give them concrete evidence that their giving has an impact. They want regular updates about successful projects and programs. They want to know who they helped. A survey performed by the Millennial Impact Report found that six in 10 millennials wanted nonprofits to share stories about successful projects and programs and appreciated information about an organization's cause and the people it serves. Most millennials look to the organization's website to find this information. In the same survey, three out of four donors said they were turned off when a nonprofit's website had not been updated recently.

The charity:water organization is a leading nonprofit when it comes to developing graphics and widgets for donors to track their investment and impact. Its website includes several tools that clearly articulate impact data. Donors feel comfortable donating to this organization because they know that they will be provided with follow-up data and can see the results that their contribution created.

The "Water Projects" section on their website tracks individual fundraising campaigns, then connects donors to an ever-updating stream of information. For the purpose of this book, I looked at charity:water's report on the campaign for a new drilling rig called Yellow Thunder.

The campaign kicked off in September of 2011, captured over 13,000 individual donations and raised a total of $1.2M to cover the rig. For me, the success of this campaign revolves around promises of transparency made by the organization, backed up by past performance of similar efforts. "We promised when the rig was on the ground, we'd track it on a map and show you proof of it in action. Here, you can follow the rig's activity and see all the fundraisers and donors who made it possible," reads the online report.

Embedded within the report is map tracking the location of the drill rig. Donors can log on to the website and track their investment. In this case, they even know the geographical location of their contribution. Other important features of the report include a video of the rig drilling its first well. This video brings a sense of satisfaction to donors as they see the actual impact of their donation down the road. All of these features make donors see their contribution more positively; if they know that they will get this kind of information and have results shared with them, new donors are going to give and existing donors are going to want to invest in as many projects as they can.

Nonprofits have to address the millennial issue. It is critical that the organizations recognize the changing landscape of donors and evolve to their giving style, because they are eager and willing to give to the right cause. For this generation, the right cause is one that they know can deliver results. Nonprofits have to make impact data more accessible to donors through their website. Simply having a tab dedicated to their annual reports isn't enough; millennials want the data to be easily accessible and engaging. Nonprofits will also have to transition their fundraising efforts toward a population that wants to make smaller, monthly contributions and requires a sharing aspect to project their social image.

PART 3

TECHNOLOGY IN USE

CHAPTER 8

BUILDING A COMMUNITY

LEVERAGING SOCIAL MEDIA

What happens in the digital space can and does have a real-world impact.

Brian Kamanzi found himself among thousands of other university students in South Africa, not in class but the streets, protesting. Brian and other students were protesting a proposed 2016 increase in the cost of university-level education in South Africa. He is a master's student attending the University of Cape Town. The protests, though, started at the University of Witwatersrand in 2015.

In 2015, students were facing 10.5 percent increases in tuition costs. A significant increase for sure, but another impetus for movement was the long-standing issue that higher education had long been too expensive for the vast majority of the South African populous. At the time, tuition was around $3,300. In 2016, Brian was facing another tuition hike to $3,700. This may not seem like much to those in the U.S. where income is extremely high and tuition costs are astronomical, but for Brian and those in South Africa where the average annual income was $6,600 in 2016, this price was a real barrier. Students argued that education was only available to the children of the wealthy and excluded South Africa's young black population, perpetuating colonial and apartheid-era problems. Indeed, research from the South African Institute of Race Relations estimated that only the wealthiest 5 percent of the South African population could comfortably afford college for their children.

The protests began with demonstrations on the campus at Wiwatersrand. Students started using the hashtag #FeesMustFall to through social media to join the outcry. Soon, students were posting photos and planning times and locations for more protests. Demonstrations sprang up at universities across the country. After securing a reduced 6 percent increase in tuition, students brought zero percent increase demands in a demonstration at the South African Parliament. Videos of riot police using pepper spray and stun grenades on the students were shared instantly via social media platforms. Posters were able to group the content and contribute to a more focused voice using the hashtag. This use of social media gave greater notice to the movement; Deprose Muchena, Amnesty International's director for Southern Africa, issued this statement following the protest: "We are alarmed by reports of police officers using teargas and rubber bullets against peaceful protesters. Students have a right to express their grievances peacefully and police must respect this right."

Brian and other students were reunited in use of the hashtag once again in 2016. Tuition fees would reportedly be increased by 8 percent for the year 2017. The #FeesMustFall movement remained joined together via social media after the incident at the Parliament and was ready to roll out once again.

However, this social media campaign was not perfect. In 2016, universities cut off Wi-Fi during the protests. The main benefit of the digital movement was the ease with which everyone could show up, volunteer, document and share everything that was going on in order to help the rest of the world better lend a hand; the high cost of mobile data was hampering students' ability to do so. The cost was a constraint to the already cash-strapped students. Being able to afford data began to limit students from sharing their vital information.

"The students on the ground need to document this movement to the world," thought Ruark Ferreira, co-founder of Ekaya Technologies. Ruark developed a truly millennial way to help these students share their message via social media. He established a website where people could remotely donate 100 MB data packages to the students at protests. All a donor needs is a Gmail account and the link to a donation form.

"You then login to your Internet banking or mobile banking app and buy a 100MB data bundle for one (or more if you can) student. Donors manually use online banking to buy airtime for the students," says Ruark. The online donation platform makes it easy for donors to quickly give. The website also accepts bitcoin donations to make giving more accessible to millennials. No third party is involved and donors directly purchase the data packages for protestors, fostering a transparent giving process. Both those willing to donate and those looking for data rushed to the site and thousands of transactions were connected. What happens in the digital space can and does have a real-world impact. Protests, fueled by social media, managed to convince Finance Minister Pravin Gordhon to set aside $1.2 billion to help cover the increases for those who needed help, those on the national student financial aid scheme.

This story illustrates the importance of participation within a digital space for the success of movements. For many organizations, it is difficult to get volunteers to physically show up to make a difference. In today's age of technology and social media, volunteers are increasingly found behind the screen. Not only are millennials willing to become fundraising advocates for nonprofits through social media, they are willing to more actively help online.

Social media use across the globe is astounding. The volume of tweets and number of users continues to climb every day. It can be extremely valuable to project your message through social media. In creating a free hashtag campaign or Facebook page, nonprofit organizations enable uber-social millennials to give them free marketing. The online sphere can also serve as a free digital meeting place, such as in Cape Town.

When effectively used, tweets and Facebook posts can provide extremely vital information. Nowadays, almost everyone has a phone, and all those phones are connected to some social media platform. For many people in need, mobile phones and social media are the easiest and most reliable avenue to receive help. The United Nations recognized the depth of information created by this vast and active network and believed it could use it to structure its aid delivery.

In December of 2012, Typhoon Bopha devastated the coast of the Philippines. It made landfall on the island of Mindanao, a large southern island rarely hit by typhoons in the area. Many communities there were remote and unprepared. As the death toll almost reached 100 on that first day, the United Nations needed help to identify regions and neighborhoods that required aid. However, the volume of tweets, over 100,000 within the first 48 hours of touchdown, proved difficult to deal with and it was hard to find actionable data.

The United Nations decided to tag in the Digital Humanitarian Network in an effort to maximize the workforce sifting through information. The Digital Humanitarian Network connects formal, professional humanitarian organizations to informal and remote yet skilled digital volunteers. These volunteers possess the skills to complete complex digital tasks on their own time. The DHN represents the millennial generation: always connected to their phones and social media, always striving to make a difference.

The U.N. wanted DHN to collect all the tweets, tag the ones that had relevant pictures or videos of damage and geotag that media. All of this would be used to create a map highlighting the most devastated areas. However, they wanted all this information within 12 hours. Patrick Meier with DHN didn't think it would be possible given their resources. So, he needed a tool to get more volunteers working on the project.

He turned to micro-tasking. Micro-tasking refers to a series of small tasks, which together, comprise a large unified project, and are completed by many people over the internet. They utilized a free and open-sourced, cloud-based platform to involve many additional volunteers. This new technology allowed the organization to expand its volunteer resources; you no longer had to be a certified contributor to the DHN. The cloud-based nature of the platform made it available to literally anyone with an internet connection. Now that's reach.

"The next morning, as our colleagues in the United Nations were waking up in Geneva, we had processed over 20,000 links, with hundreds and hundreds of pictures and video footage that we had also geotagged," Patrick remembers. As a result of the incredible work the vast network of volunteers had accomplished, the United Nations was indeed able to create the first-ever U.N. crisis map, entirely made up of crowd-sourced social media information.

Back in 2012, this was an amazing accomplishment, tackling such a vast trove of information. However, since then, big data has gotten even bigger. As mentioned before, social media today is growing ever larger. The Internet of Things is collecting more and more information in new and better ways.

Patrick Meier believes that digital humanitarianism and digital volunteers are the key to accessing and activating this data for common good. In a 2013 TedxTraverseCity talk, he said, "Clearly, these micro-tasking approaches are very powerful, and will become even more relevant for the future of disaster response. They help us to manage and filter this ocean of zeros and ones, this big crisis data." In partnership with the United Nations, Meier started MicroMappers in 2013. MicroMappers allows anyone to become a digital volunteer. Capitalizing on the benefits of micro-tasking, Meier has tapped into a mind-bogglingly large network of volunteers.

"Haiti was a game changer," says Paul Conneally, public communications manager for the International Federation of the Red Cross and Red Cross Societies. The 2010 earthquake killed over 300,000 people, left 1.2 million others homeless and left the capital, Port-au Prince, in ruins, rendering governmental organizations without the ability to act.

However, it was not these factors that made Haiti different from other disaster relief projects in the past. By 2010, people's social media and technology use had matured to the point where large volumes of relevant and accessible user-generated data could be collected. But, at the time, aid agencies and other nonprofits did not know how to make sense of or activate the vast amount of data. Indeed, at that time in Haiti, one of the poorer countries in the world, around 80 percent of people had mobile devices.

"It was really really challenging for many reasons, but in part because I think this was our first battle with big data—what I call big crisis data," says Patrick Meier, who, at the time, worked for Ushahidi. "We had hundreds of volunteers monitoring social media and news online and then we had set up this SMS platform to crowdsource text messages from disaster-affected communities in Haiti and we were just completely overwhelmed. We had this huge backlog of tweets, of text messages, that we never really were quite able to catch up on."

In addition, when they were able to process some of the information, they did not have appropriate channels for activation of the data. Many people would text or tweet where they were and what kind of help they needed, but they couldn't just give it to the right people; they didn't know who the right people were. Patrick remembers, "They would say...information that was really helpful to people on the ground, but we being a two-person team sitting in the communications department in Washington, D.C., we didn't have a clear way of dealing with that information"

Paul Conneally decided to do something about it. He wanted to find a way to leverage the incredible use of mobile and SMS technology. They partnered with Voila, a local telecomm provider, to create the Trilogy Emergency Response Application. An easy-to-use platform for two-way communication, where the organization can not only share its information with those who need help, but also where it can listen to what those people need. Outside of Haiti, the program was used in a seven-day disaster preparedness campaign; 6 million text messages were sent and received. They also used TERA to send out 1.1 million early warning texts in advance of Hurricane Thomas.

The results have been extremely powerful. The use of this new program created great impact, according to data from the organization. Of the people targeted to receive the information, 74 percent got the data and 96 percent of them thought it was useful. Empowered by the data, 83 percent of recipients took action based on the information. In addition, 73 percent of them shared the information with friends and relatives, further expanding the reach of the program.

After seeing these numbers, Paul Conneally was even more convinced that digital participation and humanitarianism would be important moving forward. In speaking on the power of social media and mobile technology and its impact on nonprofits, he said, "Technology is transformational. Right across the developing world, citizens and communities are using technology to enable them to bring about change, positive change, in their own communities. The grassroots has been strengthened through the social power of sharing."

The world is a social place. For the majority of the global population, social media has become the most important source of news, entertainment, you name it. Participation numbers on social media platforms are astronomical; this is a demographic that nonprofits have to meet to be successful.

Social media is an incredible marketing tool and discussion board for any cause or organization. A presence on social media platforms can bring a nonprofit organization a large segment of new potential donors. In addition, loyal followers and contributors of a cause can engage in discussion on social media. This discussion can lead to further increased exposure, or these people can meet up and create real change in the physical world.

Social media is valuable to nonprofits because of its reach. But this same reach can also be a tool. When so much of the population is connected to the world through social media, that quickly becomes the best place to spread important information. If your organization needs to respond quickly or send urgent information, social media is the tool to use.

CHAPTER 9

WADE THROUGH THE MUD

USING VIRTUAL REALITY TO DRIVE AWARENESS

Virtual Reality was developed as a means of entertainment to give consumers an escape from the real world and transport them to magical and different ones. Nonprofits are starting to adopt the technology for the opposite purpose, using VR to build awareness by immersing users in the reality of underwater pollution, third-world refugee camps and other situations they would be unable to experience otherwise.

Indeed, those experimenting with the technology say it is more accessible than ever before, and offers the best medium to date for evoking genuine empathy for their mission, whether it be medical research, global education or humanitarian relief.

Medical research nonprofit, Alzheimer's Research UK released a virtual reality experience that puts a potential donor in the shoes of someone living with the condition. The experience is described like this, "You meander around the supermarket loading a basket with goods—breakfast tea, sugar, milk. Along the way, though, you become befuddled. You struggle to recall the items on the shopping list. When you arrive at check out, you discover several items in the basket that you do not recall picking up. Then it comes time to pay the cashier and you can't seem to count out the proper sum." Their belief is that by making the disease and its effects more salient, the potential donor will be more likely to donate.

More so than static videos, photos or presentations, the 360 view of VR gives engages donors in a shockingly lifelike understanding of why their contributions are necessary. "VR works harder for us than any other medium," said Timothy Parry, head of brand for Alzheimer's Research UK. "You can put people right in the middle of the issue you are dealing with, something a conventional camera can't quite do."

Millennials require an increased sense of involvement in giving, so it can be hard to capture donations from individuals who are not particularly passionate about the cause or have experienced it firsthand. In addition, millennials tend to integrate causes they care about into their daily routine and purchasing behaviors, rather than making random or one-off donations. VR continues to become more affordable and commonplace within daily routines, affording nonprofits a greater opportunity to connect with millennial donors in their day-to-day activities.

An increasing number of nonprofits are turning to virtual reality as it becomes more effective for them as well. In fact, I recently attended an event where a small gift for guests was a free VR headset. Now, this device wasn't even close to the sophistication of one of the Oculus headsets. It was a simple plastic glass, connected to a piece of plastic that could flatten or lengthen accordion-style. But it worked. I could slide my phone into the back of it, turn on virtual reality videos on YouTube and watch through the plastic glass. It was so interesting to me because I had never seen VR as so accessible.

However, there are other ways in which VR campaigns can help capture more donations and broaden the impact of your organization. First, you can highlight the severity of a problem, however obscure, especially when words alone cannot convey how worrisome the problem has become. For instance, many people are still under the impression that climate change won't cause problems in their lifetimes and they don't feel compelled to take action to stop it. In an effort to change perspectives and show how urgent this issue is, the Sierra Club created the first-ever VR video about climate change, narrated by Jared Leto. The footage puts viewers in the heart of the Arctic and takes them through immersive experiences that indicate how climate change's far-reaching effects are already taking place.

As mentioned before, virtual reality technology can be used to make people more empathetic. If people don't feel connected to nonprofit organizations, they're not likely to give their time or money to support them, and creating connections can be difficult if the individuals do not have firsthand experience with certain situations. When individuals watch VR videos or play games that make the situations faced by others more real to them, they may be more likely to be empathetic and more willing to donate to a good cause that helps others.

Jeremy Bailenson has been studying the impacts of VR on empathy in his Stanford University lab. One interesting study shows how immersive experiences can affect our actions afterwards; the study put a buzzing joystick in participants' hands, mimicking a chainsaw as their virtual hands sawed down a tree. Afterwards, when an experimenter pretended to accidentally knock over a glass of water, those who had sawed down a virtual tree reached for 20 percent fewer napkins than those who only read a passage describing a tree being cut down.

Finally, these VR experiences can more clearly show donors exactly how the nonprofit is helping others. Spreadsheets, statistics and PowerPoint slides often just don't resonate when nonprofits try to tell donors how their money is used. Recently, some organizations have relied on VR to fill the void. Oculus, the maker of virtual reality headsets, developed the VR for Good program to help fund nonprofits and provide them with the resources necessary to develop creative virtual reality experiences. "A lot of times people want to see where their money is going but you can't offer them that," says Lauren Burmaster, head of the program. "That's the first thing we're really seeing—nonprofits using this technology to bring their donors to the work that's happening."

However, virtual reality is not going to be the solution for all nonprofit organizations. VR is not just a trendy new way to view content. It's an entirely new medium with a unique way of transporting the viewer into a different place and time with emotional and sometimes unexpected results. The immersive nature of VR requires that content creators apply an ethical lens to their plans before whisking viewers away to another world. "VR is like uranium," Bailenson says. "It can heat homes and it can destroy nations." The technology possesses the power to influence us to give and do good but also can prod us toward something worse. For example, Leaf Van Boven, a social psychologist at the University of Colorado, performed a study that revealed that when people are blindfolded or asked to navigate in a wheelchair, they end up with greater sympathy for people with impaired vision and mobility. However, because they experienced their own fumbling attempts to navigate an unfamiliar condition, they tended to come away thinking blind and wheelchair-bound people are less able than they actually are.

There are a few best practices to ensure that, if you do create a VR campaign, it successfully reaches and engages with donors.

In 2015, former U.S. President Bill Clinton embarked on a journey to East Africa; he witnessed children hearing for the first time, met with Tanzanian women who were selling solar energy to support their families and visited a Nairobi classroom where technology helped children learn about malaria prevention. What was unique at the time is that it was all captured in virtual reality. Since the debut of the video at the Clinton Global Initiative in 2015, as one of Facebook's first 360 videos, "Inside Impact: East Africa" has immersed more than 1 million people around the world in President Clinton's and Chelsea Clinton's 2015 journey to the region.

"The opportunities are immense for VR as a vehicle for storytelling. But navigating any emerging medium comes with its challenges," says Bryan Mochizuki, director of marketing for the Clinton Global Initiative. "I've found myself sharing four lessons based on CGI's experience as an early adopter of VR."

The first lesson is to treat it differently than traditional video and media. Organizations lose the ability to manage what the audience consumes frame-to-frame. For example, the average shot length of 2.5 seconds in modern films could nauseate your audience if applied to VR; the genre lends itself more to a long unfolding video more similar to a play or video game than a traditional web video. Also, storytelling skills are still essential in this form of media. Not every story will translate into a transformative experience through VR, so it is still important to craft an engaging narrative. The best experiences usually encompass a series of scenes that are participatory, intimate and immersive.

Another tip is to partner with the right people. While most organizations do not possess the resources to hire several different video and media teams, it is useful to look for other organizations that specialize in the area. Mochizuki explains, "At CGI, we find that collaboration in marketing and communications leads to better results as well. For 'Inside Impact,' Felix & Paul Studios, pioneers in live-action VR, provided technical and directorial expertise, while Matter Unlimited, a creative agency focused on social impact, offered storytelling and creative guidance. And our ongoing philanthropic work with Solar Sister, the Starkey Hearing Foundation and the Discovery Learning Alliance provided us with the real-life material to make a virtual yet compelling piece of art."

CHAPTER 10

BIG DATA, BIG IMPACT

USING OUTCOME DATA TO GROW

Imagine walking into one of the poorest areas of a developing country. You walk into a house there, more like a shack. You notice that there is no floor, save the dirt floor itself, and there is no running water. It may be tough to imagine but that is what it is like for many, many people in the world today. There is no electricity to power a clock, refrigerator or television. You may be shocked by everything they do not have; but you might also be surprised to know of something that they do have in this severely underdeveloped area: Coca-Cola.

"Coke is everywhere. In fact, when I travel to the developing world, Coke feels ubiquitous," observes Melinda Gates, co-founder of the Bill and Melinda Gates Foundation. Indeed, it is staggering to think about the 1.9 billion servings of Coca-Cola sold across the world every single day. Coke has achieved significant sales volumes in many developing countries, which some would have thought lacked the resources or infrastructure to be leading consumers. In fact, a lot of these places lack access to clean drinking water, so people drink Coke instead, which leads to health problems. "And so when I come back from these trips and I'm thinking about development, and Im flying home and I'm thinking, 'we're trying to deliver condoms to people or vaccinations,' you know, Coke's success kind of stops and makes you wonder: How is it that they can get Coke to these far-flung places?"

Something that it can make you wonder is, how can nonprofits achieve the same impact? Nonprofits stand to benefit greatly from observing commercial best practices in adoption of technology. Some of these practices may actually alter their external perception as "nonprofit" organizations, but can still expand impact and maintain progress toward the stated mission.

How can Coca-Cola deliver its product and its mission to places that seem so hard to reach or to service? In 2010, Melinda Gates had noticed that Coke had already found the treasure trove that is big data. At that time, Coke was already collecting and implementing real-time data from production and distribution to sales and customer feedback. One thing that big data allows it to do is change decisions and strategies as the company goes. If sales in a certain area drop, Coke notices right away and can attempt to address the issue.

In comparison, without the harnessing of big data, evaluation of nonprofit projects and movements usually comes at the very end. Often, these evaluation meetings are the first time that organizations have collected and get a chance to look at the data, and at that point, it's useless. Melinda remembers, "I had somebody from an NGO once describe it to me as bowling in the dark. They said, 'You roll the ball, you hear some pins go down. Its dark, you cant see which one goes down until the lights come on, and then you can see your impact.'" Oftentimes, nonprofit organizations are not looking at data until the money has been spent already with less than desirable results.

Big data turns on the lights. In the same way that Coca-Cola has rode a wave of continuing success after activating big data, nonprofit organizations stand to benefit. Streamlined and amplified forms of data capture or collection can help nonprofits to more actively measure the organization and its impact to help it grow. Nonprofits can piggyback on the strides made by companies exactly like Coca-Cola. The practices and ideas that they've created can be commonly used. Today, Coca-Cola continues to invest heavily in its data capabilities through technologies like artificial intelligence and the Internet of Things. It will be increasingly important for nonprofits to look at for-profit companies like Coca-Cola to find the most useful technologies and the best practices to help grow their mission.

The Internet of Things refers to the process of connecting everyday objects and appliances to the internet. This creates a network built into the activities of our everyday life. Many objects are already part of the IoT and are very recognizable. The Apple Watch and Fitbit are two wrist sensors that can track things such as heart rate, steps taken, as well as GPS location. The technology created by this network allows us to better track and assess live human data, which then allows us to streamline and improve other tasks. Massive amounts of data have already been collected by the growing network. In 2015, Gartner calculated that around 4.8 billion devices were connected to the internet. However, what is really shocking is that Gartner also estimated that by 2020, that number will skyrocket to 25 billion devices.

The private sector has readily adopted big data and utilizes that data to analyze key business decisions; I mentioned Coca-Cola in particular earlier. Much has been made about the personalization offered by corporations in the private sector, such as Amazon and Facebook. This personalization has been achieved because of their deep utilization of the IoT data network.

In fact, charity:water has created its own IoT digital tool to drive investment. Beginning in November 2015, the organization implemented a fundamentally new remote sensor network across 3,000 wells in Africa. The sensors, funded by Google at $105 per unit, were part of its efforts to increase transparency and sustainability in the water sector. Measurements recorded by the sensors include the level of water in the main well and the amount of water coming out of the spout. These metrics not only help the organization to predict potential maintenance needs and problems, but, more importantly, they also directly show donors exactly how much water their contributions have helped to deliver to communities in need.

Increasingly, nonprofits are being forced to recognize the shift toward big data. In a recent donor engagement study conducted by Abila, a nonprofit industry software provider, 53 percent of donors consider the top priority in money giving situations to be knowing where their money is going. Donors want hard, scientific data; GuideStar, another information service, published a similar report concluding that 74 percent of individual donors believed that financial statements were the most valuable reports to show donors.

This trend does not exclude other types of donors. Foundations, as well, are searching ever more for real-time data and strong statistical representation of impact. A report on foundation giving found that 90 percent most wanted to see estimates of expected impact, and 73 percent felt that reports on past performance were crucial in decision-making. "All donors are asking for metrics," says Jackie Gordon, senior vice president and chief human resources officer of YMCA of the USA. "All want some way to convey to their stakeholders how they spent those dollars—even corporate foundations."

Money for Good estimates that high-performing nonprofits could increase charitable contributions by $15 billion if they could effectively collect and present their performance data. Nonprofits, to demonstrate the necessary scientific outcomes, need to invest in enterprise resource planning softwares and other technology tools that help them analyze various and specified aspects or steps within the program. Another route for nonprofits is capitalization upon advancements made in the Internet of Things and other systems within the private sector that have affected donor engagement business making decisions. The first step for nonprofits is to distinguish which data available through the IoT is best applied to their individual mission and impact.

Kevin Barenblat, co-founder of nonprofit startup accelerator FastForward, told me that he does not see constrictive overhead levels as a problem. He believes that partnerships and networks of specialists within the social impact sector will eventually take care of the technological development and innovation. This trend is visible within the nonprofit landscape now that there are certain organizations whose missions are to aid and develop other nonprofit organizations. Some of these organizations offer Software as a Service.

SaaS gives nonprofit organizations cheap and tailored technical solutions that can help them collect and interpret actionable data. There are many SaaS startups creating and offering great solutions to today's complex social marketplace. With so many choices available, nonprofits will be able to focus on identifying solutions tailored to their mission and operations.

SaaS is also increasingly providing greater flexibility and ease of use to small- and medium-sized nonprofits. Selecting a group of services to pay for on a subscription basis is drastically different from a cost perspective than establishing and developing an in-house IT infrastructure. In addition, it is now more simple for someone to find the tool that they are looking for. Gartner Vice President and fellow Daryl Plummer expands on the topic in saying, "Budgets are being decreased and the business units are already going out and buying SaaS without talking to the IT departments about it. They're finding that they get more choice, they get it faster, they get it with less hassle—it's instant gratification if you will."

A report on key industry trends within SaaS estimates that by 2019, about 90 percent of all mobile data traffic will be generated by cloud solutions. I have also seen the effect of increasing SaaS usage. In fact, it was through one cloud platform, GoogleDrive, that the extent of SaaS use at DC SCORES was made evident. On my first day at the organization, the communications director shared with me the drive containing vital organizational information. In sharing the drive, he highlighted one particular file containing the account information and passwords for all of our subscription services. To my surprise, the list went on for seven pages; we subscribed to hundreds of services. What made it all the more surprising was that almost all the services were necessary for day-to-day tasks and campaigns.

It became extremely clear to me at that point that these services were integral to our efforts at the organization. Without this specific collection of services, we would not have the resources or technology to similarly achieve our mission. In addition, we do not have the capital resources available to develop similar tools. The expanding market of SaaS solutions can increasingly make more missions viable and impactful as they fill key holes in underdeveloped IT systems.

One very important aspect of transparency for nonprofit organizations is outcome data. Of the nonprofits surveyed, 81 percent are required to provide outcome data to their funders. When surveyed on software usage, 35 percent only use Microsoft Excel. Only 31 percent of all respondents rated their satisfaction as "satisfied" to "extremely satisfied" with their outcome management software.

One alternative to Microsoft Excel as it relates to outcome data is ETO, a SaaS platform tailored to nonprofit organizations. ETO was built with the intention of relating efforts to outcomes, ensuring service delivery is helping you achieve intended outcomes. The data which ETO generates can help you understand the effect of all your interactions so you can use valuable resources wisely in achieving your mission.

"When I started work in social change and technology 15 years ago, it wasn't a widely-held position that robust technology systems could transform mission-based organizations. More and more, I think organizations are recognizing the value and everyday uses of technologies like cloud, mobile, and CRM. However, this recognition alone won't move the needle," says Steve Anderson, former CTO of Grameen Foundation, where he lead the use of mobile and cloud technology to help alleviate extreme poverty around the world.

""What work is our organization doing, where are we doing it and how are we delivering on our mission?' These were some of the first questions I asked in 2013 when I signed on to lead the technology team at the Grameen Foundation," recalls Andersen. There were no answers to his questions. At Grameen, he had run into the unfortunate reality created by the starvation cycle. Although the foundation had grown its program greatly, at any time, it now had up to 50 projects running concurrently in eight countries, each project with its own team, goals, partners and timelines requiring precise execution.

The foundation decided to ignore cries for decreased overhead spending and invested in new technology. It built and transitioned to an IT system that enabled 100 staff worldwide to better manage its projects; it also enabled the foundation to review the staff rigorously every month against metrics and financials, and move the organization as a whole toward better results. "This system didn't solve all our problems," says Andersen, "but it was a foundational step that provided all staff with the information we needed to move more confidently toward deepening our impact."

The Grameen Foundation invested in implementing Salesforce technology. Salesforce is a leading Customer Relationship Management platform that offers applications sales, service, marketing and other administrative functions. Grameen Foundation is a lot like the other 20,000 nonprofits that use Salesforce; it helps them to be more efficient and effective in delivering their mission. But Grameen Foundation is pretty unique in that it does not only use the platform for fundraising. It has invested in and developed a number of applications that use Salesforce technology to support their programs.

One of these applications is called TaroWorks. TaroWorks is a powerful set of mobile field force management tools. Field workers at these organizations each carry an Android phone with TaroWorks installed, and it helps them do their work in a high-quality, repeatable way that also informs headquarters with critical operational data. This is important because they can do this even though they are out in very remote and rugged places gathering the data or doing tasks and servicing equipment with the goal of making people's lives better. More than 80 social enterprises have used the TaroWorks mobile application to support 170,000 micro-entrepreneurs and improve the lives of more than 3 million poor beneficiaries.

"At Grameen Foundation we use a lot of platforms, and build a number of products. We are at our core a very practical organization. We're focused on how to empower the poor to create a world without poverty," says Andersen. Indeed, the foundation's investment in technology has multiplied positive impact across the globe. Their mobile agriculture tools have enabled more than 470,000 poor farmers in Africa and Latin America to increase their productivity and earn more for their families. More than 5 million people have received health education and services through MOTECH mobile health technology, used by organizations and governments in 15 countries to address multiple needs, from improving HIV treatment to education on reproductive health. Also, nearly 500 organizations in 40 countries have used the Progress out of Poverty Index that the foundation developed to measure their poverty reduction and to improve their strategies for serving disenfranchised communities.

"Technology like this has the potential to elevate the sector, to streamline operations internally for nonprofits and funders alike. For these social impact organizations to do their jobs well and keep up with the pace of the modern world, they need information and technology systems to decide what do, track what they're doing to validate it's working, and continuously improve." Andersen does not fail to recognize the fortunate position in which Grameen found itself, though.

"Smart investment in technology requires knowing what you're trying to do. Whether you're a grantmaker or a nonprofit, it's important to take a close look at the mission you're delivering on, and asking what information you need on a daily basis to know if you're successful," says Andersen. This may seem like a simple step, but it is vitally important to see a return on investment.

To know if an organization is truly delivering on its mission requires measuring outcomes across many efforts. This makes it important for nonprofit organizations to invest in technology that can drive organization-wide outcomes. "Single-use technology systems can be put in place to solve individual problems, but a robust, integrated platform is key to measuring results across the entire organization," suggests Andersen. In addition, organizations should choose a platform that is tailored to multiple of They technological details. They should use philanthropic dollars to invest in a platform that is easy for nonprofits to use and support. Nonprofits can spend donations to build additional programs onto existing platforms on features that deliver mission value, making resources go further.

CHAPTER 11

BLOCKCHAIN FOR GOOD

THE MANY BENEFITS OF THE LEDGER

Ogoniland, an area in southeastern Nigeria along the coast of the Gulf of Guinea, has borne the brunt of over half a century of oil drilling and spills in the Niger Delta caused by oil company Shell. As a result, this is one of the most polluted regions in the world. The pollution has destroyed the livelihoods of farmers and fishermen in surrounding villages; creeks, swamps and fishing grounds are painted black by the crude oil. The spills have also devastated Nigeria's palm oil plantations, which used to provide the country, the world's top palm oil exporter, with its main export. Jobless youth face bleak futures; taking up arms, destroying pipelines and wreaking other havoc. Damaged pipelines have led to more oil spills, while corruption and locals' deep distrust of outsiders have further hampered assistance.

In 2011, the United Nations Environment Program released a report on conditions in the area. The report revealed that individuals in the region were drinking water that was contaminated with benzene, a carcinogen, at 900 times the amount that was considered safe. In addition, the report estimated that some areas could remain contaminated up to 40 years after a spill, even after cleanup efforts. "The report blew the door wide open about how bad the oil spill problem was," said Chinyere Nnadi, co-founder of Sustainability International. "When I found out about it, I knew I needed to solve this problem."

"I'm personally invested in it because it's my family history," Nnadi says in an interview with Knowledge@Wharton, the Wharton School of the University of Pennsylvania's business journal. His whole family felt invested in finding a way to create change. In 2012, Nnadi's mother, dean of diversity and inclusion at the University of Central Florida, approved a new technology developed by one of her graduate students. The program harnessed hydrocarbon-eating bacteria to clean up oil spills. The only byproduct of the cleaning is oxygen.

However, Nnadi had seen from those visits that many other groups that had tried to clean up the region had failed. From his unique perspective as an insider, he explains, "From the outside, it looks like it's something as simple as solving an environmental problem. But then, when you look into the society, you realize [the root of the problem is] systemic corruption and the lack of transparency within the actual community.... Because that system is sick, and the actors don't trust each other, no work is able to be done."

Transparency is an issue here. For any organization to truly create an effect, it would have to work around the deep-seated corruption in Nigeria, where officials have pocketed aid money in the past. To solve the problem, Nnadi said he realized that "we would have to introduce a new way of doing things." The answer: blockchain.

Nnadi hopes to combat corruption, distrust and a general lack of transparency in Ogoniland by utilizing the blockchain to create "smart contracts." "Our thesis is that because the centralized institutional nodes of accountability have been compromised, distributed accountability could be the way to serve the interest of all of the community stakeholders: citizens, government, and businesses," he says. These smart contracts bypass corruption by automatically executing payment only when all parties have fulfilled their duty. For example, if Shell has set aside $10 million to clean up an oil spill, funds would be released to the contractor after the work has been verified as finished. The work is verified by locals in the region who use mobile phones to access the blockchain and post pictures or descriptions of cleanup efforts.

A blockchain is a decentralized virtual ledger where records and transactions can be recorded, cannot be changed and are publicly available. On a blockchain, transactions are recorded chronologically, forming an immutable chain, and can be more or less private or anonymous depending on how the technology is implemented. The ledger is distributed across many participants in the network—it doesn't exist in one place. So, all entries are verifiably and trustworthy. Sustainability International is working with software company ConsenSys to develop its technology through its Blockchain for Social Good Campaign. "The reason that the blockchain is really important is because people don't need to trust each other, they need to trust the tool," says Ben Siegel, ConsenSys impact policy manager.

Shell is no millennial donor; in fact, it's a massive corporation, but transparency is still key in its social impact investing. Often, the company is obligated to pay for its spills. However, because of the lack of transparency, its investments create little to no impact. Shell craves transparency and accountability to make improvements to its giving strategy. Shell wins because it can monitor from afar and "know what's happening deep in the jungle in the Delta."

The community benefits from transparency as well because the capital invested by Shell can be better assigned to projects that create real change in the region. Locals in these communities benefit further from the implementation of the blockchain, as they are finally able to protect themselves through use of the blockchain. "You're engineering accountability," Nnadi explains. "Suddenly, you're introducing new skillsets to the community where they're able to monitor projects at international sustainability standards."

Blockchain allows nonprofits to track investments and impacts. The nature of blockchain technology is unchangeable, so it is a safe place for data storage and tracking. Another powerful use of blockchain technology is to provide a trackable identity or tag.

The Amply project will use a distributed ledger blockchain to improve the documentation system in the network of state-coordinated centers. Founder and CEO Shaun Conway offers a clearer perspective, "Imagine that, as a child, you are not allowed to play a game because you can't prove who you are. Millions of children face this every day. But it is not a game: It is the difference between being left out of the chance to learn, develop and be healthy – or to be included in life's opportunities. Amply is changing this by giving every child a digital identity that proves who they are. With Amply, children can access benefits that they are entitled to receive. For instance, Amply is enabling children in South Africa to get subsidised pre-school education, by proving that they exist and that they are attending class. This is a simple, but important start to greater possibilities."

Amply is unique in that it places each individual child at the center of their relationships with early childhood development services in a way that is "self-sovereign" and directly beneficial to them. This means that a child's digital identity and personal data are privately owned and controlled by the individual or their guardians. Over time, the identity records can become a rich source of data for the program and government organizations and can provide them with insights that can help to create more predictive, precise, personalized, preventive and participatory services.

UNICEF granted the startup $100,000 for the field experiment with a number of blockchain-based services at the country's 50 child centers. UNICEF spent much of 2017 asking the question of whether blockchain can assist in its mission of improving the lives of children across the globe. The agency's work with the technology forms part of the broader effort within the U.N. to apply blockchain in various use cases.

"The investment from the UNICEF Innovation Fund will help improve Amply's data analytics, reporting, and information management capabilities for early childhood development. These improvements will be crucial for scaling-up the application platform in South Africa. It will also enable us to share Amply's platform with international partners, other regions and also to adapt this to new use-cases that could benefit children in other parts of the world," explains Conway.

The organization ran a test program for the Decentralized Blockchain Application in some early childhood development centers over the course of two weeks in January of 2017. This was the third iteration of the DApp and the first time they tested it with a large group of early learning centers. The initial kickoff event included 10 ECD centers in Cape Town.

The program and the application of blockchain technology were effective, but Amply certainly ran into issues implementing such a system in the area. A team member from Amply stated, "Starting to test such a powerful mobile solution out in the African reality is an incredible experience. Not only does it make one realise the harsh realities we are trying to change, it also boils all the technological advancement of mobile technology and blockchain down to one factor: the user."

Coming from an industry where one boggles their mind over cryptographic principles and consensus protocols, engaging with a user and explaining the potential of a self-sovereign digital identity system is incredibly humbling. The complexity of the program can cause difficulties, especially in areas where people are unfamiliar with blockchain. It could be difficult to get someone to use or trust a program if they do not understand the underlying tools or drivers. In an effort to combat this issue, the team has been iteratively deploying new versions of the app, assisting users through a WhatsApp group in their own South African dialects and visiting them in the field to experience firsthand how the technology is working for them.

Early results from the test have been extremely promising though, simplifying administrative tasks for the centers from the start. To receive the small but vital subsidies from local government, these ECD centers apply for subsidy payments on a quarterly basis. Compiling the quarterly report includes a daunting amount of paperwork; working through bureaucracy and a submission process is prone to errors. So says Veronica Nicholas, the principal of the iThemba Early Childhood Development center in Muizenberg, Cape Town, "Sometimes we travel all the way to the department just to find an error on the form requires us to re-do the quarterly report. Sometimes the paperwork gets lost at the department and we need to re-submit."

The Amply mobile app offers an easy solution to this arduous process. The app uses the digital identities to automatically gather attendance data from each ECD center and submit it to the Department of Social Development. This is a huge step forward for the network as a whole because, before, there was no process in place to track children, whether they are attending services or at which center they were receiving services. And, as mentioned before, the department's back end system was paper-based and very little data could be gathered and analyzed in a central location to provide information about the quality of services.

CHAPTER 12

HI, HOW MAY I HELP YOU?

INTEGRATING ARTIFICIAL INTELLIGENCE

"In 2007, my best friend and partner was killed by police."

"The police said they thought he had stolen a car. He had not," Anderson soberly recalls. "He was in the hospital for some time. They beat him first. They killed him." The experience inspired Anderson to become a dedicated community organizer.

Brandon D. Anderson built a chatbot powered by artificial intelligence, Raheem.ai, that gives the public a way to grade police interactions as easily as they would rate and review a product on Amazon. With funding from Silicon Valley accelerator FastForward and an initiative called My Brother's Keeper started by President Obama, Anderson is taking the tech approach to this problem.

"Police departments crunch huge amounts of data today," he told CNBC, "but we still don't know how often law enforcement officers have hurt, killed, or for that matter saved and comforted people in the line of duty." The lack of data and transparency contributes widening rifts between police and the communities they promise to protect. This is especially true in communities of color.

People access Raheem.ai through Facebook Messenger on smartphones or via the company's own website. The chatbot asks users to answer simple questions about a police interaction, covering everything from basic details about where and when it took place to more qualitative aspects, such as whether the officer made you feel "heard" or "disrespected." The bot asks users to select from a checklist of options but allows room for some details to be submitted through written answers.

"We created this to allow city governments and different agencies to measure the performance of law enforcement through the perspectives and lived experiences of real people, especially people of color," Anderson said. "At the same time, we want to give data to organizations on the ground to help them unify around particular policy recommendations."

Raheem.ai anonymizes all the data it collects so users can be as candid as they like without fear of retaliation. The startup plans to publish quarterly reports showing where police are working well or failing communities across the United States. It will also deliver custom reports to precincts, cities or campuses to help them pinpoint areas for improvement, Anderson said.

Artificial intelligence is the new tech craze, and everyone wants in. From self-driving vehicles to Alexa, our lives are slowly transforming as a result of constantly changing and improving AI. Advancements within artificial intelligence have trickled their way downstream to the nonprofit sector. As foreign as the technology might seem to the nonprofit world, some nonprofits, including Raheem.ai, UNICEF and charity: water, are already taking advantage of AI in the form of chatbots. Chatbots can help people who struggle with reading and writing to fill out complex forms or walk them through difficult processes.

As nonprofits explore chatbots as part of their technology strategy, many reach the same conclusion: Chatbots are definitely a game changer in terms of content delivery, customer service, fundraising and user satisfaction.

AI systems do not only grant the benefit of conversational interfaces to nonprofit organizations, but paired with other key offerings, such as machine learning and computational ability, the technology can fundamentally change the sector. They can help transform donor relationship management from simply a system of record to a system of intelligence and analysis.

For example, Gravyty, a predictive analytics service, is working to impact the fundraising process. Gravyty is less an artificial persona but more of a workplace tool. The software utilizes the vast network of donor data available to nonprofit organizations. This data set is considered one of the richest because of the constant updates of donor profiles occurring at each donation. Unfortunately, this data is underutilized. Often, the data is presented in a way that appears useless to end-users and frontline fundraisers.

However, the super-powered AI-based applications can effectively sort through this vault. Predictive systems like Gravyty can sift through the information to make and relay data-informed decisions to those fundraisers. These decisions boost donor acquisition and improve existing relationships by correctly identifying which donors are most likely to give soonest, as well as what specific stories will more greatly impact an individual. Gravyty's application accomplishes this by utilizing the aforementioned conversational side of

AI; the system creates first draft, highly personalized emails to donors.

It is important to acknowledge the benefit to fundraisers offered by this data compression. End-user busy work is drastically decreased when so much of the personalization and data combing is performed by an application. This frees up time for the fundraisers to be more creative and engaging, helping to drive donations further. Indeed these AI platforms are not meant to become the next generation of fundraisers; rather, they are meant to serve as a tool to help fundraisers better achieve their goal. In many cases, platforms such as Gravyty, have been seen to increase donor acquisition tenfold.

The mission of the Cure Alzheimer's organization is now more relevant and crucial than ever before, as death rates from Alzheimer's have increased by almost 55 percent between 1999 and 2014, the CDC reports. The organization recognized the importance of innovation, to solve problems and to ask questions; how could Cure Alzheimer's help their frontline fundraisers better utilize their existing data to scale their fundraising efforts and reach more of the top donors?

In July of 2016, Gravyty partnered with Cure Alzheimer's Fund to empower their frontline fundraisers with artificial intelligence technology. By leveraging Gravyty's AI applications combined with a multipronged fundraising strategy, fundraisers at Cure Alzheimer's were able to increase total giving by 43 percent between July 2016 and July 2017.

Since partnering with Gravyty, Cure Alzheimer's has also been able to increase its average gift size by 34 percent. With algorithmic ask amounts based on dynamic and constantly changing data points, frontline fundraisers are asking for gifts best catered to each specific donor. Laurel Lyle, Director of Fundraising Programs at Cure Alzheimer's was attracted to this feature, calling it a "detailed focus on data to analyze and give it back to the frontline—giving data without complexity to the [fundraising] process."

Further importance is given to fundraiser time allotment given the current landscape of donations. The top 10 percent of the donor pool makes up 90 percent of the total donations. When fundraisers are caught up in busy work or have prioritized other donors above certain high-level donors, they are missing out on key donations from individuals who are ready, able and willing to contribute.

The market for AI tools and applications is expected to explode in the next three years. By 2020, revenue generated from AI-based systems is expected to hit $47 billion, a drastic jump from the $8 billion it generated in 2016. AI platforms can step in here to help fundraisers better prioritize attention to donors and recognize the exact time when a major donor might start to think of making another contribution.

There's huge appetite among the general public to use AI tools; according to a HubSpot survey, 86 percent of people are interested in trying them out. When given the scenario, 57 percent of respondents were interested in getting real-time answers from bots on a company website. Nonprofits need to continue efforts building on these their chatbot capabilities.

Artificial intelligence also allows you to create predictive models at a level of quality and sophistication that was previously out of reach. Nonprofit data science teams should be aware because AI can generate new opportunities: foremost, to sift through the information to make and relay data-informed decisions to fundraisers. But deep learning also enables new approaches to solving very difficult data science problems: text summarization, for example.

If you were asked to guess the words people use when they're most at risk for suicide, you'd be right to think of obvious nouns and verbs like die, overdose and, yes, the word suicide itself. So when Crisis Text Line, a free mental health support service, launched in August 2013 and built an algorithm to flag high-priority texts, it included those among 50 words to indicate the person messaging desperately needed help.

But would you guess that the word ibuprofen was 16 times more likely to predict the person texting would need emergency services than the word suicide? Machine learning and artificial intelligence can help the organization's staff sift through their troves of data to find actionable, understandable facts like that one. For this reason, Crisis Text Line integrated artificial intelligence into their algorithm in 2016. In the past, it's been literally impossible to comb through and code transcripts with suicide attempt survivors at the same scale as Crisis Text Line, which can now effectively analyze its 22 million-message database.

Another highly predictive type of content wasn't even a word, but a crying face emoji. When people included that character in their messages, Crisis Text Line supervisors were 11 times more likely to call 911 for assistance. In total, Crisis Text Line has integrated 9,000 new words or word combinations that indicate a high risk.

Artificial intelligence provides a plethora of solutions to nonprofit technology issues and questions. Machine learning can provide data science teams with striking and important alerts and facts. These data points can help nonprofits both to show donors and funders robust outcome data and to provide staff with strategic decision-making aid. Another interesting feature of deep learning is that organizations can create chatbots that can communicate in shockingly humanistic ways.

Chatbots can communicate with donors to deliver effective fundraising and walk individuals through complicated forms and processes, which usually, in turn, give nonprofits more data with which to make strategic decisions.

CHAPTER 13

ZIP CODE 2.0

WHAT3WORDS MAPPING TECHNOLOGY

"As the malarial parasites swarmed through my blood, it felt as if a war was raging inside my body. I went through two weeks of hell; sweating, hallucinations and fever. The slightest sound had my head pounding. I thought that I was going to die."

Jeremy Wade, expert angler and fisherman, recounts his battle with malaria on his Animal Planet series River Monsters. According to the World Health Organization, mosquito bites result in the deaths of more than 700,000 people every year.

In2Care developed a trap that not only kills visiting mosquitoes but also contaminates them so they kill others. In2Care is a nonprofit using the technology to work to eradicate malaria by distributing mosquito traps and nets in over 30 countries, from cities like Miami to extremely rural areas in east Africa. When mosquitos visit the trap to lay their eggs, a powder attaches to the mosquito's legs and is then transported to other breeding sites where the powder then kills larvae. In2Care is also using an eave tube for malaria mosquito control in several countries in Africa. These are simple PVC tubes built into the previously open eaves between the roof and walls of houses that mosquitoes enter when in search of blood. The tubes are closed with a fine piece of netting treated with insecticide that kills any mosquito that enters.

However, houses need to be visited twice a year to have the netting in the eave tubes retreated with insecticide, but they are often hard to find, either in the dense forests or wide open savanna areas. Johan Knols, a field operations manager at In2Care says, "Usually, when I'm trying to find someone's house, they'll guide me by saying, 'after the fourth tree, down the path to the left' or something like that." The mosquito traps need to be serviced at regular 6 to 8 week intervals to maintain effectiveness but are best placed among dense foliage, which means they may be hard to find. Both systems present logistical nightmares for service personnel.

The simple communication of location is essential for the effective maintenance of both of these systems, but that is a real challenge. Geocoding system what3words is making this communication possible by helping nonprofits reach communities in critically rural areas as well as urban slums.

Knols feels like what3words provided In2Care the breakthrough it needed, "Juggling with GPS coordinates was always a nightmare and prone to errors when being copied. With what3words, there is no way even personnel with minimal training can miss out on finding the right spot where we need them to be. It is a massive step forward for finding places in parts of the world where street names and house numbers don't exist."

"Addresses aren't designed for 2017": That is what British entrepreneur Chris Sheldrick was thinking when he co-founded what3words. "I used to work in the music business with concerts in the UK and around the world. I had the classic problem of giving an address to 50 people who all have to arrive in the same place through different methods of transportation. Addresses and postcodes were invented a long time ago and they were used for sorting mail. Now we type them into smartphones," notes Sheldrick. So Sheldrick created what3words, an innovative private company driving growth and change within the nonprofit sector by dividing the world into a grid pattern of 57 trillion 3-meter-by-3-meter squares and giving each one a unique three-word address.

"It is really starting to catch on as people realize its effectiveness," comments Rhys Jones, chief marketing officer at what3words. We are being used for such functions as postal services in Mongolia and Nigeria. Every bus stop in Nigeria has a 3-word address. We are employed by the Glastonbury Music Festival for first-aid emergency response, because w3w can pinpoint a patient in a huge crowd. And the international delivery service Aramex has started using us across Africa and the Middle East because many addresses are so vague."

The technology provided by what3words presents the opportunity to change the address system for the better. The app can help to ensure that water facilities, refugee camps, as well as schools and other informal settlements can be found in remote locations. Not only does this help beneficiaries find where they need to go, but aid workers can, for example, find a remote water facility to monitor or fix it. The app is well-equipped for on-the-ground usage and perfect for aid delivery. You don't need to be online to access the platform; the algorithm lives inside the app on your phone and uses a GPS connection to work so even if you're in the middle of the Sahara Bush with no bars, you can still find where you need to go.

Over 300 million people in India do not have access to electricity. That's 25 percent of the population. Without electricity, people resort to burning kerosene for light, which is extremely dangerous in what are often cardboard homes. Pollinate

Energy is tackling the epidemic of "energy poverty" by supplying low-cost solar and energy-efficient lighting directly to communities in need. Families are now able to access cleaner, cheaper energy on a flexible payment plan, leading to a safer and healthier life.

The energy-efficient lighting is provided to customers via a network of local entrepreneurs called "Pollinators." These entrepreneurs are given all the equipment, including a smartphone, to install the electrical systems and perform customer maintenance visits within the slums. Before, Pollinate Energy would use GPS coordinates to locate its customers. While this may have been a better approach to defining a customer's address than "50m from the entrance, take a left and second tent on the right," using latitude-longitude pairs to communicate location is difficult and error-prone for non-technical people.

People find it easy to remember three words. The use of words means people can communicate precise location quickly, easily and with less ambiguity than with any other system. Using the what3words mobile app, Pollinators are able to find a customer's three-word address and record it with ease. Data during the visits is uploaded to Pollinate Energy's Salesforce cloud software when a connection is available. Pollinate Energy then visualizes its customers on a map along with key information such as who lives there and the impact their energy supply has. The what3words system makes this all possible; "As of right now over 45,000 individuals have benefited from Pollinate Energy's distribution, collectively saving almost 2m tonnes of CO_2." Ben Merven, co-founder and Chief Operating Officer of Pollinate Energy, said, "what3words' simple addressing system can help us efficiently service those individuals and scale the business faster."

According to the United Nations, 75 percent of the world suffers from inconsistent, complicated or inadequate addressing systems. This leaves around 4 billion people invisible; with no address, people are unable to receive mail or exercise rights as citizens.

For countries with struggling infrastructure, what3words can put an address system in place. In Mongolia, about 30 percent of the population is nomadic. This makes delivering and receiving mail an enormous challenge. Most Mongolians are forced to collect their mail from a far-away post office box, and some simply have no access to mail. The Mongol Post, the country's national mail service, switched to the three-word system. The change was viewed as an efficient and cost-effective way to improve Mongolia's postal problems in rural areas and in the capital, Ulaanbaatar, where many streets do not have names and many residents live in makeshift housing without a designated address. Putting in a sophisticated new street addressing system is a major endeavor that can require millions of dollars worth of investment and decades to put in place. The Mongolian people saved time and money by going digital.

Even in countries with an address system, problems still arise. For example, delivering parcels and letters isn't always straightforward in the Ivory Coast, where street addresses are few and far between, and the large settlements often have no address system at all. The postal service relied heavily on post office mailboxes and descriptive directions based on visible landmarks. For many people, packages came very close but never actually reached their hands.

To tackle the problem, the country adopted a new system for delivery based on what3words technology. La Poste will integrate the technology with traditional postal mapping through a smartphone app. "In what3words, La Poste has found a simple solution that instantly provides Côte d'Ivoire with a robust and multi-lingual addressing system. It will help us to extend e-commerce opportunities, home delivery and support businesses in both urban and rural spaces," Isaac Gnamba-Yao, CEO of La Poste de Côte d'Ivoire, said in a statement.

This innovative mapping platform has also proven vitally important during disaster and emergency relief efforts. The mapping technology has very quickly changed the landscape of disaster relief in the wake of Super Typhoon Haima in the Philippines.

Managing aid and logistics in the wake of natural disasters such as earthquakes, floods and hurricanes is already a huge challenge in places with a developed address systems in place. In areas where the infrastructure is incomplete and the local population relies on landmarks, the issue is exacerbated tenfold. "What happens when the meeting point, say the chapel with the red spire, gets blown away?" explains Richard Lewis of what3words. "When that disappears, the piece of land underneath where it stood still has the same address. People can still find the location needed for aid, rescue, and shelter."

"The typhoon basically wiped out all of the infrastructure," recalls Jones, "and all of the landmarks that they typically used for telling people about location. So, to assist people, they used us." The Red Cross has already seen firsthand how effective the app is, enabling it to help the residents of Luzon when Haima struck, causing up to $76.9 million in damages, killing four and displacing more than 100,000 people. Jones explains, "The app is either used by first responders, as a form of infrastructure to direct and move people and responders around, or it can be used by people who are affected by the situation. They can use it to tell people where they are. But being able to say, 'I am here,' or, for them to say, 'You guys need to get to this location, this is a safe zone,' is a simple, useful way to move people about."

This technology is going to be key for nonprofit organizations to drive growth in developing nations. With their slim infrastructures, even well-strategized philanthropic plans fail to deliver impact. So many people get stuck out in "no man's land." With what3words, now you can actually find them and give them what you have to offer.

CHAPTER 14

DELIVERING IMPACT

INNOVATIVE USES FOR DRONES

Night has fallen at Liwonde National Park, Malawi, but the trespassers are still clearly visible. Three hundred feet in the air, a thermal camera attached to a BatHawk drone tracks their boat, a black sliver slicing over the luminous gray Shire River.

"They're breaking the law by coming into the park," says Antoinette Dudley, one of the drone's operators, pointing to her computer screen.

More than two miles away from the boat, she and her partner, Stephan De Necker, are seated in their Land Cruiser and command center. A monitor attached to the driver's seat displays the drone's vitals, and another behind the passenger's seat streams live video from the camera, operated with an old PlayStation console.

"Let's give them a scare," says De Necker. With the tap of a few keys, he switches on the drone's navigation lights and sends it beelining toward the boat. The reaction is instantaneous: The boat makes a U-turn, high-tailing it out of the park.

Africa is in the midst of a profound poaching crisis: The continent's elephant population declined by 30 percent from 2007 to 2014, much of it because of poaching. At least 1,338 rhinos were killed for their horns in 2015 alone. Liwonde, in particular, has lost about 50 elephants and two rhinos since 2014 to poachers. Not to mention the fact that criminals are becoming increasingly militarized in their tactics, and efforts to stop them have thus become more dangerous and complex. In August 2015, the Malawi Department of National Parks enlisted the help of African Parks, a nonprofit that specializes in rehabilitating struggling protected areas.

The nonprofit has plenty of tried an true tactics; since taking over operations in Liwonde, the group has confiscated upwards of 18,000 illegal snares, made over 100 arrests, installed more than 60 miles of electric fencing and removed 261 elephants to another reserve.

African Parks' unusual experiment with high-tech, calling in a drone team from South Africa, is an interesting development for the organization. With funding from the World Wildlife Fund, including a $5 million grant from Google, drones are being tested here in the first systematic evaluation of their potential to combat poachers.

Drones are becoming increasingly important for organizations of all types and sizes. Many drone applications already exist, but many more will certainly arise over the next few years. The word "drone" might inspire images of counterterrorism strikes and the future of package delivery. But quadcopters and other autonomous flying vehicles are just yet another new and emerging technology revolutionizing the ways we tackle the biggest social and environmental issues of our time.

Drones are superb for visual data collection. They are perfect for wildlife conservation, search and rescue, and understanding what is needed in disaster relief. Even low-cost hobbyist drones like the Parrot AR drone quadcopter, which runs at around $150, can produce and send high-definition videos and photos to a smartphone or tablet.

There are several use cases wherein nonprofits can benefit from advancements in drone technology. The visual and recording technology available in drones today can provide organizations with extremely powerful geographical mapping data for conservationist or disaster relief purposes. Nonprofits can also use this stunning aerial footage as effective marketing material; the footage appeals to millennials, similar to virtual reality videos.

The delivery capabilities of drones are highly touted; for-profit companies like Amazon are spending millions to develop a drone delivery arm. Nonprofit organizations can use these small devices to transport and deliver small, yet vital pieces of medicine or information. Nonprofits like Zipline are showing just how disruptive and effective this technology can be.

In Rwanda, a young woman starts bleeding after giving birth by C-section. Try as they might, her doctors can't stop the bleeding. They've already transfused the two units of matching blood that they had on hand. They could call the national blood bank in the capital of Kigali to request more, but ordering it and sending it the 25 miles over mountainous roads to the hospital would take up to four hours. The woman doesn't have that kind of time.

Doctors call a distribution center near Kigali, where clinic workers and a flight crew load a series of small, unmanned aircraft with the needed supplies and launch them into the sky. Within 45 minutes, they have dispatched seven units of red blood cells, four units of plasma, and two units of platelets, more than circulates through the entire human body. Each drone needed just 15 minutes to reach the hospital, where it dropped its payload on a predetermined landing zone. Emergency staff were able to collect the supplies and use them to stabilize the 24-year-old patient.

Delivering medical supplies by drone has become almost routine in Rwanda since the California startup Zipline arrived in October 2016. "We do this every day," says company founder and CEO Keller Rinaudo.

Zipline is expanding into neighboring Tanzania, establishing the world's largest national drone delivery service. The Tanzanian government wants to make as many as 2,000 daily deliveries from four distribution centers serving an area roughly the size of Texas and Louisiana. While Zipline might expand further in Africa, Rinaudo believes its services could be useful globally. "Rural healthcare is a huge problem in the US too," he says. For reference, the organization has so far performed 1,400 deliveries in Rwanda with a squad of around 60,000 drones.

For the new service, Zipline plans to fly upgraded versions of its fixed-wing drones, which have a 6-foot wingspan and can cruise at 70 mph. Each can carry 3 pounds of cargo—one unit of blood weighs roughly 1.2 pounds—and the batteries can make a round trip of 100 miles. Folded wax paper parachutes and cardboard cargo bays make the drones both durable and cheap to operate and repair. "The new vehicle is highly modular," says Rinaudo. "If a sensor is giving weird readings, it's super fast to replace that."

An estimated $6.4 billion is currently being spent each year on developing drone technology around the world and that figure is expected to double to $11 billion by 2024. Also within the decade, Teal Group analysts estimate the total amount spent worldwide on research, development, testing and evaluation of drone technology will reach $91 billion.

UNICEF officials said forming relationships with international governments and the price of using drones are obstacles that need to be overcome. "It's still more expensive to use a drone in Malawi than it is to pay somebody to take [supplies] on a motorbike," said Chris Fabian of UNICEF's Office of Innovation and Ventures.

San Francisco-based Otherlab recently launched the world's most advanced industrial paper airplanes to do just that. The APSARA glider is made of biodegradable materials and can carry more than two pounds of lifesaving supplies, such as blood and vaccines. When dropped out of a cargo airplane, the drone's interior tech helps it steer itself in a spiral motion to a designated location using GPS and autopilot. It can land within a 33-foot radius of its intended destination.

While drones are often chastised as indiscriminate killing machines in Afghanistan and Syria and feared by privacy advocates in the United States, drone use has skyrocketed around the world in recent years. There are now at least 700,000 in the United States alone, according to Bard College's Center for the Study of the Drone, which, since 2012, has been tracking trends with drones, also known as Unmanned Aerial Vehicles. Hundreds of companies are now producing drones around the world.

Zipline makes a habit of recruiting and training local engineers, health workers and flight operators to de-escalate any of the suspicion or worry that people have with drones. As was the case in Rwanda, Rinaudo knows his team will have to work with local communities to emphasize that the aircraft perform humanitarian, not military or surveillance, work.

However, drones can do so much more than just deliver medicine and record video. Even with technology so innovative, the people behind the organization still have to get creative.

For decades, government agencies and nonprofit organizations have tried to prevent the spread of mosquito-borne diseases that kill million of people each year in developing countries. In the past, they have tried spraying large areas with insecticides, but that process is expensive, especially as mosquitoes begin to develop resistance to commonly used chemicals.

The United States Agency for International Development has begun to look for other mosquito control methods. One approach is to breed male mosquitoes in captivity, expose them to radiation that renders them sterile, and release them into the wild. In large enough numbers, the sterile males will outcompete wild males for female mosquitoes, which can reduce local populations by as much as 90 percent. This method has been around for half a century, but spreading sterile mosquitoes in the developing world is a challenge. Roads are nonexistent or in poor condition, so it may not be possible to release insects from a car or truck, and using a crewed aircraft is too expensive.

In 2016, USAID funded an organization called WeRobotics, which has dual headquarters in Washington, D.C., and Geneva, Switzerland, to engineer a system that can deploy sterile mosquitoes from autonomous drones instead. USAID and WeRobotics want to see whether drones can replace conventional aircraft as a way to manage mosquito populations over hundreds of square kilometers.

Klaptocz and his colleagues started WeRobotics to explore ways that drones can have a positive social impact. Over the past few years, they've set up community robotics labs in developing nations around the world. WeRobotics and its partners have used drones to map roads in Nepal, deliver medicine in Peru and coordinate humanitarian efforts in the Caribbean after Hurricane Maria. The company's latest project is testing a prototype drone-based mosquito control system in South America.

What is interesting here is that the nonprofit organization is facing a challenge not with the drone itself, but rather in how to carry and release mosquitoes from that drone. "Mosquitoes are very fragile animals," Klaptocz explains. "If you put hundreds of thousands of them into a very small box, they're going to damage themselves, and damaged mosquitoes will not be able to compete with wild mosquitoes." The trick, according to Klaptocz, is to keep them inside a precooled container: "Between 4 °C and 8 °C, they'll fall asleep, and you can pack them up fairly densely."

The organization also has a public perception hurdle to tackle, WeRobotics must work with local communities to win their support. "We're trying to control disease vectors," Klaptocz explains. "But practically, what we're doing is releasing a whole bunch of mosquitoes into communities and flying drones over them. Engagement with these communities has to be done from the beginning, by talking to people and involving them in the process."

It's not yet clear that drones will be much more effective at dispersing mosquitoes than humans with backpacks, says Robert Malkin, an expert on new health care technologies at Duke University. And sustaining any kind of operation in remote areas with little infrastructure will be a challenge. "But it could work," he says. "It sounds like a cool project."

It does sound like a cool project. The potential impact created by this innovative new strategy is huge. Drones, like other forms of technology, possess unique characteristics and tools to help nonprofit organizations to greatly expand their impact and accelerate their mission delivery.

Drone usage can be useful for many different kinds of nonprofits. Depending on their missions, organizations can develop and customize drones to do what they need them to do. These devices can be used for surveillance, mapping, video recording, small-object delivery, you name it. Nonprofit organizations should brainstorm to discover any potential usages they might have for a drone in the ranks.

REFERENCES

Kamanzi, Brian. "#FeesMustFall: Decolonising Education." Africa | Al Jazeera. Al Jazeera, 03 Nov. 2016. Web. 26 Feb. 2018. <https://www.aljazeera.com/indepth/opinion/2016/10/feesmustfall-decolonising-education-161031093938509.html>.

William Foster, Alex Cortez, Katie Smith Milway. "Nonprofit Mergers and Acquisitions: More Than a Tool for Tough Times." The Bridgespan Group. N.p., n.d. Web. 26 Feb. 2018. <https://www.bridgespan.org/insights/library/mergers-and-collaborations/nonprofit-mergers-and-acquisitions-more-than-a-too>.

"What3Words: How Three Words Are Making The World A Safer Place." The Ethicalist. N.p., 17 Aug. 2017. Web. 26 Feb. 2018. <https://theethicalist.com/three-words-making-world-safer-place/>.

Paynter, Ben. "Demanding That Nonprofits Not Pay For

Overhead Is Preventing Them From Doing Good." Fast Company. Fast Company, 03 June 2016. Web. 26 Feb. 2018. <https://www.fastcompany.com/3060455/demanding-that-nonprofits-not-pay-for-overhead-is-preventing-them-fro>.

Lamb, Paul. "Transforming the Social Sector: Bitcoin and Blockchain for Good." The Huffington Post. TheHuffingtonPost.com, 08 Jan. 2018. Web. 26 Feb. 2018. <https://www.huffingtonpost.com/entry/transforming-the-social-sector-bitcoin-and-blockchain_us_59c169e3e4b0f96732cbc9c7>.

Afshar, Vala. "How Nonprofits Can Use Artificial Intelligence To Improve Fundraising." The Huffington Post. TheHuffingtonPost.com, 28 Sept. 2017. Web. 26 Feb. 2018. <https://www.huffingtonpost.com/entry/how-nonprofits-can-use-artificial-intelligence-to-improve_us_59ccf9efe4b02ba6621ffacb>.

Moeti, Koketso. "Digital Activism Comes Of Age: Technology Is Creating New Space For Marginalized Voices." The Huffington Post. TheHuffingtonPost.com, 18 May 2017. Web. 26 Feb. 2018. <https://www.huffingtonpost.com/entry/digital-activism-comes-of-age-technology-is-creating_us_590b498ae4b046ea176ae884>.

Beal, Adam M. "Funding the Future: Social Enterprise on the Rise." The Huffington Post. TheHuffingtonPost.com, 02 May 2016. Web. 26 Feb. 2018. <https://www.huffingtonpost.com/adam-m-beal/funding-the-future-social_b_9825656.html>.

Aug 15, 2017. AfricaMiddle East & Africa. "Using the Blockchain to Clean Up the Niger Delta." Knowledge@Wharton. N.p., n.d. Web. 26 Feb. 2018. <http://knowledge.wharton.upenn.edu/article/using-blockchain-clean-niger-delta/>.

Ruiz, Rebecca R. "4 Cancer Charities Are Accused of Fraud." The New York Times. The New York Times, 19 May 2015. Web. 26 Feb. 2018. <https://www.nytimes.com/2015/05/20/business/4-cancer-charities-accused-in-ftc-fraud-case.html?_r=0>.

"Virtual Empathy: How 360-Degree Video Can Boost the Efforts of Non-Profits." Nielsen, 2017. Web. 26 Feb. 2018. <http://www.nielsen.com/us/en/insights/news/2017/how-360-degree-video-can-boost-the-efforts-of-non-profits.html>.

Ken Berger, Jacob Harold and Art Taylor. "The Overhead Myth." Non Profit News | Nonprofit Quarterly. N.p., 30 June 2015. Web. 26 Feb. 2018. <https://nonprofitquarterly.org/2013/06/17/the-overhead-myth/>.

Conway, Marian. "Blockchain Offers Nonprofits a Software Solution for Accountability." Non Profit News | Nonprofit Quarterly. N.p., 21 Aug. 2017. Web. 26 Feb. 2018. <https://nonprofitquarterly.org/2017/08/21/blockchain-offers-non-profits-software-solution-accountability/>.

Haider, Don. "Nonprofit Mergers: New Study Sees Strategy and Success." Non Profit News | Nonprofit Quarterly. N.p., 22 Feb. 2017. Web. 26 Feb. 2018. <https://nonprofitquarterly.org/2017/01/11/nonprofit-mergers-look-contexts-indicators-success/>.

Mirchandani, Bhakti. "How to Save a Nonprofit: The Care Steps Required in Mergers and Acquisitions." Non Profit

News | Nonprofit Quarterly. N.p., 28 July 2017. Web. 26 Feb. 2018. <https://nonprofitquarterly.org/2017/06/20/how-to-save-a-nonprofit-mergers-acquisitions/>.

Elliott, Justin. "How the Red Cross Raised Half a Billion Dollars for Haiti and Built Six Homes." ProPublica. N.p., n.d. Web. 26 Feb. 2018. <https://www.propublica.org/article/how-the-red-cross-raised-half-a-billion-dollars-for-haiti-and-built-6-homes>.

Eng, Monica. "Watchdogging the Charity Watchdogs." The Seattle Times. The Seattle Times Company, 29 Dec. 2011. Web. 26 Feb. 2018. <https://www.seattletimes.com/life/lifestyle/watchdogging-the-charity-watchdogs/>.

Eckhart-Queenan, Jeri, Michael Etzel, and Sridhar Prasad. "Pay-What-It-Takes Philanthropy (SSIR)." Stanford Social Innovation Review. N.p., 2016. Web. 26 Feb. 2018. <https://ssir.org/up_for_debate/article/pay_what_it_takes_philanthropy>.

Brandt, Julie. "Overhead Costs: The Obsession Must Stop (SSIR)." Stanford Social Innovation Review. N.p., 2013. Web. 26 Feb. 2018. <https://ssir.org/articles/entry/overhead_costs_the_obsession_must_stop>.

Haider, Donald. "Nonprofit Mergers That Work (SSIR)." Stanford Social Innovation Review. N.p., 2017. Web. 26 Feb. 2018. <https://ssir.org/articles/entry/nonprofit_mergers_that_work>.

Gauss, Allison. "Why We Love to Hate Nonprofits (SSIR)." Stanford Social Innovation Review. N.p., 2015.

Web. 26 Feb. 2018. <https://ssir.org/articles/entry/why_we_love_to_hate_nonprofits>.

Lee, Louise. "When Nonprofits Act Like Businesses, Transparency Improves." Stanford Graduate School of Business. N.p., 2017. Web. 26 Feb. 2018. <https://www.gsb.stanford.edu/insights/when-nonprofits-act-businesses-transparency-improves>.

"A New Way to Judge Nonprofits: Dan Pallotta at TED2013." TED Blog. N.p., 06 Oct. 2014. Web. 26 Feb. 2018. <https://blog.ted.com/a-new-way-to-judge-nonprofits-dan-pallotta-at-ted2013/>.

Qua, James. "IoT Entices New Donors at Nonprofits." The Wall Street Journal. Dow Jones & Company, n.d. Web. 26 Feb. 2018. <http://deloitte.wsj.com/cio/2017/07/12/iot-entices-new-donors-at-nonprofits/>.

Overly, Steven. "How Nonprofits Use Virtual Reality to Tackle Real-world Issues." The Washington Post. WP Company, 12 Oct. 2016. Web. 26 Feb. 2018. <https://www.washingtonpost.com/news/innovations/wp/2016/10/12/how-nonprofits-use-virtual-reality-to-tackle-real-world-issues/?utm_term=.16198032fd79>.

"Trustlab – Connected Development : Building Amply, a Web of Trust for Children." UNICEF Stories. N.p., 2016. Web. 26 Feb. 2018. <http://unicefstories.org/2016/11/14/9needs-connected-development-building-amply-a-web-of-trust-for-children/>.

Necula, Deanna. "UCLA Alum's Nonprofit Uses New Technology for Niger Delta Cleanup." Daily Bruin. N.p.,

2016. Web. 26 Feb. 2018. <http://dailybruin.com/2016/04/12/ucla-alums-nonprofit-uses-new-technology-for-niger-delta-cleanup/>.

Bodker, Ilana. "Virtual Reality: The New Nonprofit "Marketing to Millennials" Technique." Millennial Marketing. N.p., n.d. Web. 26 Feb. 2018. <http://www.millennialmarketing.com/2017/09/virtual-reality-the-new-nonprofit-marketing-to-millennials-technique/>.

"World's First Refugee Camp Powered by Renewable Energy from Solar Plant." IKEA Foundation. Https://www.ikeafoundation.org/, 2017. Web. 26 Feb. 2018. <https://www.ikeafoundation.org/stories/post_typestoriesp2614/>.

"Azraq, the World's First Refugee Camp Powered by Renewable Energy." UNHCR. N.p., 19 May 2017. Web. 26 Feb. 2018. <http://www.unhcr.org/ph/11769-azraq-worlds-first-refugee-camp-powered-renewable-energy.html>.

Behringer, Chase. "Want to Make Your Nonprofit More Innovative and Tech Savvy? Acquire a Startup." Medium. CMB Advisors, 15 Aug. 2017. Web. 26 Feb. 2018. <https://medium.com/cmb-advisors/want-to-make-your-nonprofit-more-innovative-acquire-a-startup-ad6c984af201>.

Dixon, Daniel Ducassi and Matt. "Brown Arraigned on Charges She Used Group to Fund Lavish Events, Car Repairs." Politico PRO. N.p., 08 July 2016. Web. 26 Feb. 2018. <https://www.politico.com/states/florida/story/2016/07/corrine-brown-fraud-indictment-one-door-education-foundation-103643>.

Pallotta, Dan. "When My Business Failed." Harvard Business Review. N.p., 23 July 2014. Web. 26 Feb. 2018. <https://hbr.org/2012/08/when-my-business-failed.html>.

Sullivan, Laura. "In Search Of The Red Cross' $500 Million In Haiti Relief." NPR. NPR, 03 June 2015. Web. 26 Feb. 2018. <https://www.npr.org/2015/06/03/411524156/in-search-of-the-red-cross-500-million-in-haiti-relief>.

Adamczyk, Alicia. "Hurricane Harvey: How American Red Cross Donations Are Used | Money." Time. Time, 2017. Web. 26 Feb. 2018. <http://time.com/money/4920070/hurricane-harvey-where-the-money-goes-when-you-donate-to-the-american-red-cross/>.

Made in the USA
Coppell, TX
06 January 2023